FIGURATIVE DESIGN IN *HAMLET*
THE SIGNIFICANCE OF THE DUMB SHOW

FIGURATIVE DESIGN IN *HAMLET*
The Significance of the Dumb Show

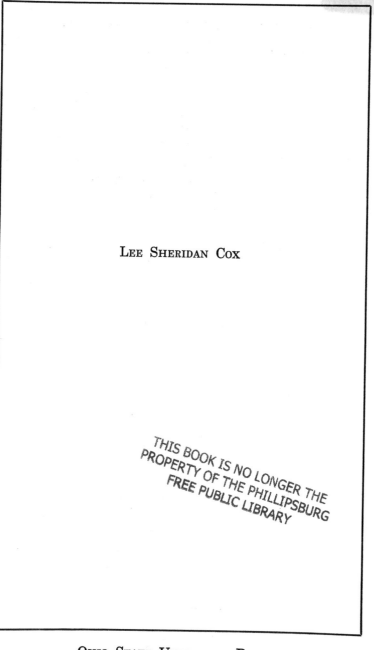

LEE SHERIDAN COX

OHIO STATE UNIVERSITY PRESS

Copyright © 1973 by the Ohio State University Press
All Rights Reserved
Manufactured in the United States of America

Library of Congress Cataloging in Publication Data
Cox, Lee Sheridan
Figurative design in Hamlet
Includes bibliographical references.
1. Shakespeare, William, 1564-1616. Hamlet.
2. Pantomime. I. Title.
PR2807.C68   822.3'3   72-12916
ISBN 0-8142-0175-X

FOR HELEN LOUISE

CONTENTS

ACKNOWLEDGMENTS

This book has been in process for a good many years, during which I have accumulated a variety of debt to a good many people. The study had its beginning in a paper written for a graduate seminar at Indiana University; and I recall, with gratitude, fellow students whose enthusiasm for my early argument enforced my own confidence in it. I am similarly indebted to friends and colleagues along the way for a stimulation that comes with good conversation and encouraging support: I must name, with a particular sense of obligation, Fran and Arnold Shapiro, who were always ready to talk about *Hamlet*, and Robert M. Estrich and Bernard O'Kelly, whose response to an early product of my argument contributed to its progress. I wish to express special gratitude to those who took time from busy schedules to read the entire book in manuscript and to give me the benefit of their counsel: warm thanks are due to John Harold Wilson and John Gabel; to Rolf Soellner, with added appreciation for his helpful critical notes on the first draft; and to Roy W. Battenhouse, whose generous and open-minded interest in the work of his students can always be counted on and whose provocative teaching and critical advice were a constructive force in the making of this book. Details and conclusions of the germinal study mentioned above were later employed in a chapter of my graduate dissertation, written in 1962 under the direction of the late William Riley

Parker. Although the latter work dealt with Milton's use of imagery and the comment on *Hamlet* served only comparative purposes and although Mr. Parker did not see the present study in manuscript, students who had the good fortune to work under his kind and invaluable tutelage must be aware, in the course of any scholarly project they subsequently undertake, of profit from his precepts and example: I record such debt in grateful memory.

The obligation of the *Hamlet* critic to the published work of others defies express acknowledgment. Some of that indebtedness is indicated in my text and notes. However, the latter are necessarily compressed and selective, intended to direct the reader to related lines of inquiry or to findings closely similar or directly contradictory to my own, rather than to provide general bibliography. It goes without saying that if this study of the dumb show helps to effect a resolution of certain long-debated questions (as I hope it does), that result has been implemented by the work of many scholars whose contributions may not be documented in these pages. Finally, I am indebted to the Ohio State University for a grant that freed me from routine academic duties in the winter of 1967; to my typist, Mrs. Roger Johnson, whose competence deserves kudos; and to the staff of the Ohio State University Press for courteous assistance and painstaking care in the editing and proofing of the text.

FIGURATIVE DESIGN IN *HAMLET*
THE SIGNIFICANCE OF THE DUMB SHOW

CHAPTER ONE

In modern performances of *Hamlet,* the dumb show is frequently omitted. Many critics have protested the deletion, some of them vigorously. J. Dover Wilson says, "Remove [the dumb show], and what happens? The play scene is ruined."[1] One may agree with this opinion and at the same time suspect that the custom of gauging the worth of the mime only by its contribution to the play-scene accounts, in part, for failure to establish the show as indispensable. Referring to the "common assumption" that the show is "only a mechanical necessity," H. D. F. Kitto says, "In a dramatist of Shakespeare's class, should we not expect the dumb-show to be . . . an integral part of the whole?"[2] Certainly, one might expect to find a special, even an intrinsic, significance in a dramatic convention to which Shakespeare gives unconventional form. And when a playwright has his protagonist, expounding on the art of the dramatist and the actor, scorn "inexplicable dumb-shows and noise"[3] although the playwright himself is employing a puzzling dumb show (through the agency of the scorner) and, repeatedly, the noise of kettledrum, trumpet, and cannon, one might suppose both the silent scene and the sound of ordnance to be germane to a large purpose. To date, one approach to the significance of the show has not been taken: a close consideration of its nature and function in the light of figurative and structural patterns throughout

3

FIGURATIVE DESIGN IN *HAMLET*

Hamlet. When Shakespeare placed the mime in the second scene of the third act, he gave it a medial position in the unfolding of the framing action. In the following study, I hope to demonstrate that he also gave it a meaning central to his basic thesis and a figurative significance that makes it inexpendable.

Midway in the course of *Hamlet* a drama in progress before the assembled court of Denmark is interrupted when the Danish King, rising from his seat in the audience, cries, "Give me some light," abruptly dismisses the players, and leaves the "theater." The dramatic matter thus violently terminated is itself violent: a ruler is treacherously slain; his place of power is then assumed and his wife wooed and won by the killer. The inner-stage performance is repetitious: what the players first enact in dumb show is in the process of replay, with dialogue, when the theater is closed by the invoker of light. And if one action is presented in two dramatic forms to the stage audience, it is thrice-presented in as many guises to the *Hamlet* audience. "The matter" that the King and the Queen of Denmark have been entreated to "hear and see" (III.i.23) and that they first only see, the *Hamlet* audience has first only heard. For both pantomime and playlet iterate the gist of the tale poured into "ears of flesh and blood" (I.v.22) by the Ghost of Hamlet's father who—appearing to Hamlet, accusing King Claudius of murder, and charging Hamlet with revenge—recounts, in vivid detail, the peculiar circumstances of that murder and its immediate aftermath: the King sleeping in the garden; the pouring of poison into the sleeper's ears; the "leperous" effect of the deadly hebenon (64); the murderer's subsequent abuse of "the whole ear of Denmark" with false report of the victim's death (36–38); his wooing of the victim's wife with "wicked wit" (44); and his success in this, as in his assault on the ears of King Hamlet and Denmark. Thus, an account of two forms of poisoning by way of the ears is first presented in affecting narration by a speaker who repeatedly enjoins his audience to "hear," to "list" (5, 7, 22, 34). His hearer then resorts to action on a stage as a medium for, and determinant of, action in the Danish court. Proposing to

4

observe the show that Claudius presents on seeing a dramatization of the deeds ascribed to him, Hamlet commissions the performance of *The Murder of Gonzago* (or *The Mousetrap*). Before the King whose "seeming" he so can "censure" (III.ii.91–92) and the court whose ear has reportedly been abused by false report, the substance of the Ghost's revelation is pantomimed in a scene that dispenses with the spectators' ears and is repeated in dramatic action with dialogue.

This play-scene has been a subject of much scholarly controversy, and perhaps no aspect of it has aroused more argument than the dumb show. There is concord among critics on one point: they all remark that the show is unconventional. Although few studies of it have taken into close account the use of the show elsewhere in Elizabethan and Jacobean drama, a commonplace of the comment on the silent scene in *Hamlet* is that it "has no parallel in Elizabethan drama."[4] But with this observation, harmony on the matter ends. Varying approaches to *Hamlet*—whether they are, for example, mechanical, philosophical, or psychological—may naturally elicit different views on the function of the dumb show. But among those scholars whose approaches are similar, opinions on Shakespeare's use of this dramatic convention differ remarkably. The range of opinion is so great that even a brief sampling of some of the interpretations attendant on varying approaches throws into sharp relief the peculiar nature of the pantomime and the questions it raises.[5]

The fact that the action of the dumb show precisely foreshadows the action of *The Murder of Gonzago* is one feature of the court entertainment that has puzzled critics and has led to considerable disagreement among them. It has been argued that the pantomimic prefiguring of the action to follow is needed, in order to inform the *Hamlet* audience of the plot of *Gonzago*, since the latter is to be interrupted. But this explanation is more often rejected than approved: it has also been frequently pointed out that there is no need for a pantomime for such a purpose, since the necessary information has already been provided in the Ghost's description of his murder, in Hamlet's declaration that he will have the players "play something like the murder of [his] father" (II.ii.624), and in his remark to Horatio that one scene of *Gonzago* "comes near the circumstance" of his father's death (III.ii.81–82). In a similar antithesis, some critics say that Shakespeare intends, by means of the silent preview, to leave the *Hamlet* audience free to watch the stage audience during *Gonzago*, and others say that the dumb show cannot be justified on such a score, since neither action nor speech in the playlet is calculated to require undivided attention from the *Hamlet* audience. Such differences of opinion do not necessarily reflect a fundamental disagreement on the importance of the pantomime. But there *is* striking disagreement on this point. At one end of the spectrum is the commentator who finds the show useless and who, looking for an explanation for Shakespeare's insertion of a useless matter, hypothesizes that an original dramatic version of the Hamlet story contained a dumb show, that Shakespeare omitted it in his version, and then that the players in his troupe insisted on its reinsertion, lest the groundlings protest the loss of a popular scene. At the other end is the critic who contends that the dumb show is Shakespeare's means for pointing to inaccuracy in the story of the Ghost, since—so the critic says—Claudius's lack of reaction to the pantomime indicates that it does not reflect his crime.

The readings are as diverse when the focus is on Hamlet as dramatist, on his intentions in regard to the pantomime, and on the part it plays in his scheme. All of the following views, with various emphases and qualifications, have been set forth at one time or another by one or more critics: the dumb show is a foolish miscalculation on Hamlet's part; it is not of his doing, but is instead an unexpected addition by the visiting players, who thus jeopardize his plan; it is a part of a careful method of providing a double test—Hamlet, being cautious and conscientious, employs both the dumb show and *Gonzago* so that the determination of Claudius's guilt will not rest on just one trial; it is one of a planned series of shocks, since Hamlet knows that Claudius will not be "caught" easily; it is an aspect of his decision to keep the King guessing, to tantalize him and increase his perplexity; or (since an exact presentation of following action is not traditionally characteristic of a dumb show) it is a crafty means of deceiving the King into a position of false security, of providing him with a sense of relief that he will not have to experience anything so close to the fact again, so that *Gonzago* will hit him with double force.

There is an accompanying variation in the interpretations of the effect of the show on Claudius. Some critics say that it puts him on guard; others, that it catches him off guard. One argues that the pantomime immediately provides the King with the information he has sought, the "source of [Hamlet's] distemper" (II.ii.55); others argue that it puzzles him. Since Claudius says nothing about the pantomime, there is perhaps more extreme disagreement on the question of his reaction to the show than on Hamlet's purpose in employing it. One may read in one critical study that the mime allays Claudius's fears; in another, that it starts the turn of the screw and leads to an exhibition of terror; in another, that it attests to his coolness and self-possession in the face of a recognized threat. The fact that Claudius does not comment on the dumb show has led to hypotheses that he is not sitting where he can see it or that, engrossed in conversation, he does not pay any attention to it, theories that have been contested on various counts—for example, the unlikelihood of the King's not having a good view of a court performance,[6] particularly one that he has been "entreated" to attend, or his ignoring one sponsored by a nephew he wants to conciliate.

Such a bare sampling does not do justice to the interest of many of the arguments in which these views appear. It does, however, reveal some of the questions provoked by the dumb show and those most commonly debated: why does the mime directly anticipate the subject matter of *Gonzago*? does Shakespeare preview the play in order to provide information? if so, is the information necessary? if unnecessary, is the show superfluous? if superfluous, was the device forced on Shakespeare against his own better judgment, or was it a politic catering to popular taste? what is Hamlet's purpose in employing the show? or is it foisted on him by the visiting players? what is the effect of the show on the stage audience? is Claudius's silence during and just after the show significant and, if so, what does it signify? Some of these questions can be dealt with more summarily than others: it has often been pointed out that the show provides suspense, develops tension, and serves (with *Gonzago*) to present an effective dramatic contrast to the action that frames it—in brief, that giving information is not the only office of a pantomime. And as to whether the show was imposed on Shakespeare by the other members of his troupe, as W. J. Lawrence conjectures, or on Hamlet by the players, as J. Dover Wilson contends, the first begs the question and the second, though part of an ingenious argument, is not supported by strong evidence.

The most important shortcoming, as I see it, in critical explorations of the nature and function of the dumb show lies not so much in the questions asked as in a failure to search for answers outside the confines of the play-scene itself. Thus, only infrequently are certain other questions surely relevant to the whole matter considered, and then only casually: for example, is Hamlet's expression of contempt for dumb shows significant in a play that includes one? what is intended by the frequent parallels, implicit and explicit, between the "puppets" in the court entertainment (or characters in a fiction) and the characters in the play proper? why have a "presenter" who is, in effect, mute insofar as any real fulfillment of the function is concerned, and a prologue that, belying its name and nature, is silent, uninformative, about the matter that follows? And many other questions also requiring that the mime be viewed in the context of the whole play have never been asked: for instance, do the reiterated allusions to "dumbness" throughout *Hamlet* throw any light on the meaning of the silent scene? does the frequent linking of dumbness and noise, in conjunction with the literal use of stage noise, have any bearing on the use of the dumb show?

Perhaps a failure to take a large view of the show is manifested in certain confusions sometimes found in arguments on its function. Obviously, though Shakespeare stands behind the whole play, one must distinguish properly between his intentions and those he gives to the dramatist within the play, between the purposed effect on the *Hamlet* audience and that on the *Gonzago* audience. An explanation for Shakespeare's use of the show must naturally be more complex than an explanation for Hamlet's use of it; one does not automatically add up to the other, and each must accommodate the other. If, for example, it is said that Shakespeare needs the pantomime to inform his audience of a plot he plans to break off in the middle, Hamlet's need for the show must still be accounted for—after all, *he* does not know that the play will be interrupted. The same considerations must apply when one is focusing on Hamlet's motives. It is true that a critical study centered on the purposes of the dramatist within the play and evoking a Hamlet who is rash or careful, inept or crafty, foolish or wise, cruel or antic or conscientious, or various combinations of these, inevitably implies that Shakespeare employs the pantomime for ends he does not share with Hamlet. Even so, in some writings, the words "Hamlet" and "Shakespeare" are carelessly interchanged, and the implicit distinction between the motives of the two is fuzzed by the explicit imprecision. Moreover, one can hardly avoid the suspicion that some scholars go so far afield in an effort to solve difficulties relevant to Hamlet the dramatist that, paradoxically, they lose sight of the dramatist Shakespeare. However convenient it may be to a solution of certain questions about the court entertainment to declare that Claudius is deep in conversation during the dumb show, it is hard to believe that Shakespeare wants his readers to arrive at such a conclusion when he gives the King no conversation and has no other character allude to such speech or action.

This hypothesis of an inattentive Claudius is suggestive in another way of a general limitation in critical writings on the matter. Dover Wilson, in declaring that Claudius converses during the mute performance,[7] is taking exception to evidence elsewhere of the King's alertness and habitual public show of good manners; W. W. Greg, in declaring that the show is used to establish the falsehood of the Ghost's account,[8] is contradicting proof elsewhere of truth in the Ghost's version of the crime. And although other commentators may not so conspicuously challenge or deny evidence elsewhere in the play, they do tend to overlook the relationship between the dumb show and figurative patterns and motifs that run through the drama. Claudius's lack of verbal reaction to the dumb show has hamstrung critics trying to determine the effect that the show has on him; and his silence *is* ambiguous if one isolates the scene. But passages elsewhere in the play have a bearing on the matter of the King's silence. There is, for example, at the opening of *Hamlet* a species of "dumb show";[9] and it, too, provokes dumbness in the spectators. The very words are used: we are told that the Ghost is "dumb" and that his appearance causes the "watch," in turn, to "stand dumb" (I.i.171;ii.206). No dumb show proper, the Ghost's appearance is yet described in terms reminiscent of traditional uses of the convention,[10] and Horatio's account to Hamlet implies that the Ghost resorts to a kind of speaking action-without-words, a "show" later attested to by stage direction and dialogue when the Ghost appears again. A pattern of key words insistently reiterated and of a particular kind of stage action consistently reemployed informs the use of the panto-mime proper. And if Claudius's dumbness in the face of the dumb show is viewed in the light of the overall figurative pattern, one may see that his silence (the only evident reaction; all else—conversation, terror, self-possession, and so on—is conjecture) is, in itself, a clue to the character of his response and a clue to the function of the dumb show as well.

I repeat what is, in my opinion, a basic matter: why does Shakespeare have a man who commissions a play containing a mime inveigh against "inexplicable dumb-shows and noise"? Furthermore, why does he have a man of taste, whose critical judgments in *some* respects reflect (in the light of Shake-speare's practice) Shakespeare's own views, express distaste for two dramatic devices that Shakespeare himself is em-ploying? The first question has occasionally caught the passing attention of a critic.[11] The second has not. And a close look at both is long overdue. No note has been taken of Hamlet's adverse criticism against the background of Shakespeare's practice and relevant comment in *Hamlet*: the use of a dumb show; the use of stage noise; the re-peated allusions to both dumbness and noise; the pro-vocative equations of the two; the insistence that both produce only more of the same. (The latter idea, to be traced and analyzed in forthcoming chapters, is suggested in a variety of ways: for example, in the descriptions—as well as the stage use—of a chain of noise in which the drum starts the sound of the trumpet, the trumpet the sound of the cannon, the cannon the reverberation from the heavens, "re-speaking earthly thunder.") Nor, in any study of Shakespeare's manipulation of the dumb show convention, has note been taken of a chain of acts (or descriptions of acts) approximating "dumb show" throughout a play that begins with the silent and "solemn march" of a dead man past the watch at the "dead hour" in "the dead vast and middle of the night" and concludes with watchers who are "mutes," with "senseless ears," a "peal of ordnance," a "dead march," and the spectacle of dumb show. Those critics who find the exact pantomimic foreshadowing of *Gonzago* so unusual should look beyond the immediate context of the scene: the matter described by the Ghost, repeated in dumb show, and repeated again in *Gonzago* (presented thrice, like Hecate's curse "thrice blast[ing], thrice infect[ing]," or like the appearance of the Ghost three times before the watch—also referred to more than once as a potential blasting and linked repeatedly with infection) fits into a pattern of repetition marked by echoing and reechoing words and noise, echoing and reechoing acts, by such insistent reiteration, in fact, that technique itself serves as indirect comment.

Let me illustrate, merely by the expedient of choosing several words or phrases much annotated but almost invariably without recourse to passages outside the play-scene, the importance of looking beyond the immediate context of the scene itself. D. G. James has said, "It is a platitude of Shakespeare study that Shakespeare could, with wonderful ease, charge a word with two or three meanings at once; there is hardly a page of Shakespeare which does not illustrate this."[12] It is also a commonplace of that study that certain familiar Renaissance themes are inherent in the *Hamlet* plot: for example, that wrongdoing recoils on the doer and that evil generates evil. And Caroline Spurgeon's study has shown that Shakespeare often connects noise with evil and the reverberations of sound with the movement of evil.[13] Given such premises

and given in *Hamlet* the stage use of a chain of noise that rit-
ualizes intemperate or violent action, one cannot consider only
in their immediate context such suggestive expressions as
"false fire" and "mallecho" (to select, from the many similarly
charged words and phrases in the play-scene, two describing
the play-within-the-play and the dumb show). Whether Hamlet, by "false fire" (III.ii.277), refers to the whole court entertainment or particularly to the representation of the Player
King's poisoning or to the promised representation of a wooing
is not really important: that the King is taunted with being
"frighted" by a mere likeness of the real thing, a blank discharge, is clear.[14] What does deserve attention is the name
"false fire" for a stage representation of evil within a larger
dramatic frame that makes repeated use of false fire in the
drinking rites to give ceremonious form to immoderate or
false action. Similarly, Hamlet labels the dumb show "mallecho" (148); unless one dismisses the possibility of wordplay,
"mallecho" is an apt name for a show that echoes the actions
described by the Ghost, if not his words.[15] Both "false fire"
and "mallecho" accommodate a meaning of evil; both link evil
with noise; both are used to describe dramatic action; both
are peculiarly applicable to Shakespeare's use of ordnance:
the blank discharge of the cannon is certainly "false fire," and
both the method used and the reverberation of the martial
sounds may be fittingly termed "mal-echo"—especially in
view of the nature of the acts transformed into noise. If such
elements elsewhere in the play do gloss these designations for
drama, then the mute scene, as well as the one with dialogue,
is called a noise and there is a suggestion of evil in the noisy
custom or the noisy stage production itself, as distinct from
the matter each represents.

Of course, two examples do not make a pattern. But when
the same figurative connections appear again and again, it is
harder to believe that they are all fortuitous, all casual, all
inconsequent, than to believe that they are not. Again without
drawing any conclusions about the purport of provisional examples of figurative interplay, let me point to one more line
in the play-scene that also contains some of the connections
potential in "false fire" and "mallecho" and that, picking up

implications elsewhere in the dialogue, may provide more details for what might add up to a comment on drama—and on the dumb show. It has been observed that Hamlet's quotation, "the croaking raven doth bellow for revenge" (when he is urging Lucianus to "begin") is "possibly reminiscent of the *True Tragedie of Richard the Third*: 'The screeking raven sits croaking for revenge. Whole herds of beasts come bellowing for revenge.' "[16] A dissimilarity in the two quotations underscores an oddity manifest in the *Hamlet* line. One wonders at Shakespeare's strangely inappropriate use of the word "bellow." Just before the play-scene Hamlet censures "bellowing" and uses the word to describe actors who lack "the accent of Christians" (III.ii.35–36); yet here he uses it in support of an injunction to a character to "act." Elsewhere, he uses bellowing" to describe players who "imitated humanity . . . abominably" (39–40); yet in a play where a pervasive bird and beast imagery illuminates a comment on beastly nature as contrasted to what is properly human and where "bellowing" is descriptive of players who do a bad job of imitating "humanity," he refers to a bellowing fowl in exhorting a stage representation of a man to action. The very unsuitability of the word in its immediate context draws our attention to it and leads us to notice its fitness in a larger context where noise is linked with various manifestations of violence and evil; both with some form of dramatic action; and men who imitate humanity "abominably" with the beastly. Also, we again are presented with a contrast between what happens in the play-scene and Hamlet's earlier remarks on drama: not only does he scorn dumb shows and then ask for a play that includes one; he also expresses dislike for "noise" and "bellowing" and the beastly, and then enjoins a player to "act" in their name.

Moreover, the form of the dramatic inset, as well as individual words and phrases within the play-scene, takes point from patterns of fact and figure throughout *Hamlet*. For example, technique provides a counterpoint to matter when an "act" of murder leads to its reenactment within a framing action where murder recurrently leads to murder.[17] And the nature of the two presentations in the inset makes the sequence of which they are a part an oblique echo of a process detailed earlier in the play. Whereas both pantomime and playlet dramatize an act described in the Ghost's tale to Hamlet and thus add up, as we have noted, to a peculiar sequence of *accounts* of king-killing, the Player's Speech —tale and dramatic performance in one—describes an *act* of king-killing as a similar sequence of sound, silence, and renewed sound. In the Player's rendition of Aeneas's tale to Dido, we hear that Pyrrhus (a son bent on avenging his father's death) directs a blow at Priam that, though failing to take the king's life, occasions his fall, an event marked by a "hideous crash" as "senseless Ilium / Seeming to feel this blow . . . Stoops to his base." This noise "takes prisoner" the "ear" of Pyrrhus; his sword "seem[s] i' the air to stick," and in mute tableau he stands like "a painted tyrant." His pause, likened to the "silence" before a storm when the winds are "speechless," is succeeded by "dreadful thunder," as Pyrrhus again turns his sword on Priam (II.ii.490–510). Thus, the slaying of a king is described as a process of "crash," "hush," and "thunder." A correspondence between a sequential description of a matter of king-killing and the form that matter takes in the sequence of the Ghost's tale, the mute scene, and the playlet, may appear to be tenuous stuff, especially when analogies between the two matters are imprecise and fluid. But references to, or instances of, sequences of sound or silence or both are too common in *Hamlet* to be called chance. One must conjure with the possibility that the pattern significantly charges the passages in which it appears.

Neither the limited purpose and effect of the dumb show nor its larger dramatic function can be determined when one views it only in relation to *Gonzago* and the stage conversation immediately framing it. One may agree with any one of various arguments supporting the proposition that Hamlet deliberately employs the dumb show: for instance, that it is consonant with his nature to bait Claudius, as cat with mouse. But within the context of the play-scene there is no absolute disproof of the argument that Hamlet does not bargain for the show. One may agree with the critic who argues that Claudius's silence accords with the response one might expect from a self-possessed man adept at dissembling, aware that a stage facsimile of his deed may be coincidence, and reasonably confident that it strikes no chord in the majority of the viewers; that such a man might naturally resort to subterfuge with the question, "Have you heard the argument? Is there no offence i' it?"; that it is consistent with Claudius's resolute, crafty, and decisive nature that though he bears with a mute and unemphatic stage counterpart of his deed and with its replica so long as no note is strongly struck that connects him in the mind of the generality with the stage villain, he acts abruptly when threat increases and the stage wooing of a dead ruler's wife is forecast. Nevertheless, within the context of the play-scene there is no absolute disproof of the argument that Claudius does not see the show or that, seeing it, he is oblivious to its purport. Given certain interpretations of cause and effect, one may agree with those who find the show an important part of a dramatic movement illuminating the natures of both Hamlet and Claudius. But given other interpretations, one may as well agree with those who find it superfluous. Within the scene itself, nothing tips the scale in a definitive way. But if one looks elsewhere in the play, one finds a pattern suggesting that dumb show is the logical issue of Hamlet's expressed intent and that Claudius's silence is the logical issue of dumb show; in short, that the mime is not a matter of accident and that Claudius does see and does react to it.

So, agreeing with W. W. Lawrence that the play-scene is "the keystone to the arch of the drama,"[18] I propose to approach the question of the dumb show from a somewhat different tack than that ordinarily taken: first, by way of a look at traditional aspects of the convention and Shakespeare's choice and use of those that serve his particular purpose, and then by a study of the part the mute scene plays in a comprehensive figurative and structural design.

CHAPTER TWO

In his careful study on the dumb show, Dieter Mehl remarks on the difficulty of "defining the exact meaning and limits of the term": observing that "any piece of silent action where one would normally expect dialogue may be called a dumb show," he adds, "However, one can usually apply the term ... to all cases where one or more characters advance and retire without having spoken." This broader definition he subsequently qualifies in classifying processionals, but he also later notes that it is often hard "to draw the line between dumb show and a particularly festive procession" or, drawing the line and saying of the processions in one play that they are not dumb shows proper, he adds that "in performance [they] possibly assumed the character of dumb shows."[1] If the boundaries of the term are not always easy to pinpoint, there remain definable variations in the form of the show: perhaps the most frequent is the "whole scene, complete in itself, without dialogue"; in another familiar form, the show may present "only a short significant gesture or a brief meeting, important for the development of the plot"; the simplest form, one common to the classical tragedies, is the ceremonial procession.[2]

Some of this may appear irrelevant to the present study. Obviously, there is only one dumb show in *Hamlet*: it is so labeled by the playwright, it meets the requirements of the initial definition above, and it takes the first form described.

But *Hamlet* also includes repeated instances of, and references to, other silent actions, some of which recall forms of the show, some of which contain allusion to "show" or "mutes" or "dumbness," and the pantomimic nature of which is often emphasized in the dialogue. And such details must, in a play where a dumb show figures prominently, give us pause; for the peculiar nature of the convention, its mobility and variety, the familiarity of the audience with its elements and uses—all provide the dramatist with conditions for evoking in the spectator imaginative equivalences between matter and technique. If Shakespeare should want to invest mute action with a large symbolic significance, he might—by a recurrent use of pantomimic actions that recall a familiar form, characteristic, or gist of the dumb show—exploit a symbolism inherent in the latter; and any resultant comment on "dumb show" might serve as a reagent to measure the dumb show proper. On these premises I propose to list instances and descriptions of pantomimic action in the play; to note whether they contain reminders of the stage convention of dumb show; to determine whether they (and passages describing or presenting speechlessness or motionlessness) present a consistent pattern of comment relevant to the play-scene; and then to consider briefly the use Shakespeare makes of ordinary components and subject matter of the stage device. The label most frequently applied to the dumb show in *Hamlet* is "unique"; and this may suggest that Shakespeare's mime has little in common with other pantomimes. But I hope to demonstrate that it is unique, not because it lacks conventional ingredients, but because Shakespeare, evoking a contemporary familiarity with those ingredients, puts common practice to uncommon use.

We have noted that the word *dumb* is assigned to descriptions of the action and effect of the Ghost (I.i.171;ii.206). And if one recalls the nature of the action that often marks a dumb show, certain aspects of the Ghost's comportment when he appears before the watch are most suggestive: for example, he "with solemn march / Goes slow and stately by them: thrice he walk'd / . . . whilst they, distill'd / Almost to jelly with the act of fear, / Stand dumb and speak not to him" (I.ii.201–6). The action of the dumb show is often similarly solemn and ritualistic; and mimes frequently show a thrice-presented action: in *Gorboduc*, for instance, the company of mourners in one of the shows passes "thryse about the stage." Thus, the accounts of the Ghost's early appearances contain reminders of a form and a formula of the dumb show; and recollection is further joggled by a repetition of the word *dumb* to describe all of the participants in these brief meetings. Then, when the Ghost appears for the first time to Hamlet, both dialogue and stage direction emphasize his speaking action, his gesturing, at the outset of the meeting: the reiterated reference to the "beckon[ing]," the "courteous action," as the Ghost "waves [Hamlet] to a more removed ground" (I.iv.58, 60–61,68,78,84) underscores the Ghost's initial resort to mute action.

In the first passage above, we are told that the Ghost's appearance causes the spectators to "stand dumb"; but in another passage, it is said and shown to produce what would appear to be an opposite effect: a "show of violence" (I.i.144). This early intimation that a dumb action may elicit both dumbness and violence (the latter itself significantly called a "show") is repeated in various ways: each piece of pantomimic action in the play has a direct bearing on the next, and each produces a show of dumbness or a show of violence, noise. Hamlet reacts with disproportionate passion when his companions try to thwart the mute summons of the Ghost; and after the Ghost tells his story, the immediate effect on Hamlet of the encounter that begins with a dumb gesturing is "wild and whirling words" (I.v.133) when he, in turn, communicates with others. Most significantly, the next time we hear of him (when Ophelia details the form of his visitation to her in her closet), he is described in words emphatically used to describe the Ghost (see, for example, I.ii.233–34) and in phrases reminiscent of earlier speculations about the "perturbed spirit": he is "pale . . . piteous . . . As if he had been loosed out of hell / To speak of horrors" (II.i.81–84). Not only has he thus put on some of the look of the Ghost; he also now resorts, like the Ghost, to dumb action. When Polonius asks Ophelia what Hamlet "said," she answers:

He took me by the wrist and held me hard;
Then goes he to the length of all his arm;
And, with his other hand thus o'er his brow,
He falls to such perusal of my face
As he would draw it. Long stay'd he so;
At last, a little shaking of mine arm
And thrice his head thus waving up and down,
He raised a sigh so piteous and profound
As it did seem to shatter all his bulk
And end his being: that done, he lets me go:
And, with his head over his shoulder turn'd,
He seem'd to find his way without his eyes;
For out o' doors he went without their helps,
And, to the last, bended their light on me.

                                        (II.i.87–100)

This account of a brief meeting composed of mute gesturing, a waving of the head "thrice," and a strange symbolic departure recalls the action of the dumb show. And, again, whatever brings on Hamlet's "dumb show"—whether it is the ghostly communication that begins with a silent beckoning or Ophelia's own silence, her refusal to talk with him or to accept his letters—there is the implication that *his* mute action is generated by an earlier action that is, in some sense, "dumb."

Similarly, the Player's Speech expands the intimation that "dumbness" may lead to "dumbness" or to "the show of violence." It does not, like the descriptions of the Ghost or like Ophelia's account of Hamlet's conduct, describe a speaking action-without-words. But besides picturing a silent tableau in the midst of a scene of "crash" and "thunder" and thus continuing the motif of dumbness and noise, the tale of King Priam's murder does detail a peculiar process of cause and effect: as we have seen, a blow (itself retributive in nature) causes a noise that effects a "pause," succeeded by "aroused vengeance." Violence is symbolized by a "hideous crash" that produces a "silence . . . hush as death": both sound and silence are elements in a process of destruction. An evil action has such consequences that its own movement is arrested, and the "pause" that ensues (likened to "silence") seems to reflect a potential for ending the process. However, in Pyrrhus's case both noise and silence reflect the nature of storm, and his "still[ness]" leads to renewed vindictiveness and "dreadful thunder." And, most suggestively, hard upon this figurative illustration of a movement of evil comes Hamlet's request that the players perform *Gonzago*, a play preceded by a silent scene. Then on the heels of the dumb show—which elicits only silence from Claudius—and the playlet comes the prayer scene.

Hamlet's conduct in Ophelia's closet may be termed "dumb show" in the sense of a mute exhibition of grief; but though Claudius's conduct in the prayer scene may include the factor of speaking action, his attitude of prayer may be, in another sense and by his own admission, termed "dumb show," whether mute or not. The reference in this passage to a "pause" and the suggestion, again, of a particular cause-and-effect process are relevant to our present purposes. Immediately after the dramatic presentation of a ruler's death, the initial part of which strikes him dumb, Claudius describes himself in lines reminiscent of the Player's description when, stricken by the crash that marks a king's fall, Pyrrhus stands in "pause" and like "a painted tyrant . . . like a neutral to his will and matter" does "nothing." Claudius now says of himself, "Like a man to double business bound, / I stand in pause where I shall first begin, / And both neglect" (III.iii.41–43). A declaration of a condition of pause follows on the dumb show and *Gonzago*, and a potential in the "crash" of the court entertainment for catching the conscience of the King or for leading to new violence appears to be suggested in Claudius's awareness of "double business." But what transpires, as shadowed forth by his words just before he kneels, is a "silence . . . As hush as death." And when he rises from prayer saying, "Words without thoughts never to heaven go" (98), he reveals that his appearance of devotion has added up to only that—appearance, seeming, mere "noise," mere "dumb show."

Moreover, the analogy is two-pronged and twice enforces the figurative comment. Like Pyrrhus, Hamlet strikes a blow, in the dumb show and *Gonzago*, which "strikes wide"; nevertheless, "the whiff and wind" of it brings the King to his knees and occasions a pause. But although the sword of the onlooker

Hamlet "stick[s]" in the air and, like Pyrrhus, he does nothing, the pause leads only to new-aroused vengeance. It, too, is death-like and is followed by Claudius's plan to have Hamlet killed in England and by Hamlet's striking a blow at an arras. Both of these blows fall wide of the mark; yet both result in "hideous crash," one the "fall" of a father whose death leads to the silent procession of Ophelia's mourners. The movement of violent action and pause, the chain of noise and dumbness and renewed noise described in the Player's Speech, shadows forth the dramatic process in *Hamlet*.

To return to instances of pantomimic action that recall types of the dumb show proper, we should note that the court entertainment is also followed by the reappearance of the Ghost, whose visitation is again pictured in terms of a speaking action-without-words. Critics offer various explanations for the Ghost's return and his declaration that he comes "to whet [Hamlet's] almost blunted purpose" (III.iv.111) at a time when Hamlet has just slain Polonius, thinking him the King. But whatever additional explanations there may be for this reappearance, it is logical—in view of a pattern wherein various manifestations of noise and dumbness produce more of the same—that the dumb show should beget various kinds of "dumb show." And despite the fact that the Ghost speaks, the scene also contains, in Hamlet's words to Gertrude about the Ghost, reference to pantomimic elements or, at the least, reminders of a "form" or "action" that speaks: "Look you, how pale he glares!" says Hamlet. "His form . . . preaching to stones, / Would make them capable. Do not look upon me; / Lest with this piteous action you convert / My stern effects" (125–29). The fact that the Ghost appears to Hamlet, but not to Gertrude, is reminiscent of an infrequent use of the dumb show: elsewhere in English drama there are shows that are visible to only one person on the stage. Although such mimes may be used to provide indirect comment on the sole viewer's state of mind[3] and although some critics have argued that the Ghost *is* a figment of Hamlet's imagination, catching an echo here of a traditional use of the device does not require acceptance of the strict implications of the use or connive at the idea that the Ghost is a projection of Hamlet's mental state. After all, the appearance of the Ghost is not a dumb show, and he is seen elsewhere by other characters in the play. But his materialization after the court entertainment, in the midst of a violent harangue, and on the words "a king of shreds and patches," and the effect of his "dumb show" on Hamlet, whose resultant "distemper" Gertrude initially calls madness, reflect the process found elsewhere in connection with pantomime or with speechless and motionless display.

The last silent actions I want to point to take the form of processions.[4] The first is so labeled: *Enter* Priests, *Etc. in procession; the Corpse of* OPHELIA, LAERTES *and* Mourners, *following;* KING, QUEEN, *their trains, Etc.* The dumb-show processional frequently presents a matter of sorrow, and the funeral procession becomes a traditional motif, used alone (as in the classical tragedies) or to begin a show (as in *Antonio's Revenge*).[5] So the filing on stage of the company of Ophelia's mourners, though not a dumb show proper, contains echoes of a familiar form and a familiar subject matter. Again, immediately succeeding this mute action is a scene of rant and violence: perhaps not only the movement we have observed, but also the figurative equivalences of dumbness and noise, are accommodated by the use of the processional elsewhere to *begin* a dumb show.

The play ends with another procession; during it a particular music that often marks a dumb-show processional is played. Horatio says, "Let four captains / Bear Hamlet, like a soldier, to the stage" (V.ii.406–7), and the final stage directions are *A dead march. Exeunt, bearing off the dead bodies; after which a peal of ordnance is shot off.* Again, a silent action is followed by a noise that is an intrinsic part of the sequence. The purpose of the procession, its ceremonious nature, the music—all recall the dumb show. Moreover, earlier, Hamlet's names for the spectators, struck dumb by what they witness, as "mutes or audience to this act" (346) recall, on the one hand, characters in a dumb show and imply, on the other, that what they watch and *hear* is a show. Thus, since the "act" is a matter of noise heard by an "audience" and since the "mutes" occupy the same sphere of action as the actors, Hamlet's speech and its context reinforce the metaphorical comment that noise effects dumbness and that dumb show and the show of violence/noise are essentially one. And it is the scene thus defined that leads to the silent scene "high on a stage."

One idea in the pattern we have been tracing—that "dumb show" or "the show of violence" breeds more "dumb show," more "noise"—bears on Shakespeare's use of repetition in the play-scene. Repetition is not an uncommon ingredient of the dumb show. In, for example, *The Downfall of Robert, Earl of Huntingdon,* after the dumb show has been enacted once, the presenter asks the players to repeat the scene, and it is reenacted while the presenter introduces each character and explains the action; in *A Warning for Fair Women,* the murder shown in a dumb show is "also presented in the actual play," and "the incident is successively presented in two different ways, once in the form of a morality, the second time as a factual report."[6] No one would argue that repetition is a technique sparsely employed in the literature of the time. The Renaissance poet is likely to say everything twice over—not to recapture the first fine careless rapture, but to impress moral ideas on reader or spectator; and he is likely to give that repetition different forms, extending and enriching his instruction by the varied nature of the repetition itself. And as the examples above from other plays demonstrate, reiteration is a natural concomitant of a dramatic convention that so often aims at explication or teaching.

But we have seen that the use of repetition in the court entertainment in *Hamlet* has touched off a puzzled response from critics. What surprises is the precise duplication, joined to the fact that the dumb show lacks the allegorical disguise so often conveying moral instruction and justifying a repetition. Moreover, the repetition does not take the common form of edifying narrative; it does not appear to serve any of its usual ends: to detail, explain, clarify, moralize, provide an enlightening change of perspective, and so on. And, at that, it goes beyond what is ordinarily remarked on: the mime rehearses an action already presented in description by the Ghost. Thus the action is given, in some form, three times. We have had occasion to notice Shakespeare's reference to the thrice-performed action: the poison used by Lucianus is "thrice blasted, thrice infected" with Hecate's curse (III.ii.269); the Ghost appears thrice before the watch, a point repeatedly insisted on; when he appears, "thrice he walk'd / By their oppress'd and fear-surprised eyes" (I.ii.202–3); the dialogue suggests that the Ghost beckons to Hamlet thrice, though this is perhaps debatable; "three times, and in vain," one critic says, "Hamlet tries to get away from the Ghost" during the "swearing" ceremony;[7] and when Hamlet resorts to mute show with Ophelia, "thrice his head thus waving up and down, / He raised a sigh" (II.i.93–94). When the same detail is attached, again and again, to an unnatural action, then technique may take on import. This is not to say that all repetition, even when it is threefold, serves the same end. The use of parallel and counterpoint is a salient feature of the drama: for example, three sons—Hamlet, Laertes, and Fortinbras—with fathers slain; three injunctions to "remember"—from the Ghost, from Laertes, and from Ophelia in madness; a scene wherein a man whose father has been murdered listens to a dramatic speech about a man who kills the father of his father's murderer. Playing off character against character, situation against situation, is a method of procedure found in all of Shakespeare's plays; and *Hamlet* contains many instances of this technique. But in the peculiar unvaried repetition in the court entertainment where the action in the dumb show leads to exactly the same action in *Gonzago*, Shakespeare gives technique itself thematic significance. Employing a familiar element of the dumb show in an unfamiliar way, he graphically illustrates the idea that "dumbness" and "the show of violence" perpetuate themselves. Technique informs the dramatic process where the story of the Ghost generates a dumb show which mirrors that story and which, in turn, is mirrored in the ensuing playlet. And in the light of the figurative process elsewhere in the play, the repetition suggests that all are "dumb shows," though two of them are variously presented with words.

The relationship drawn between noise/violence and dumbness is also indebted to the traditional character of the mime. Noise is a common ingredient of the silent scene. Sometimes the stage directions call simply for a background "musicke" (see, for example, *Endimion*); sometimes, more specifically, for trumpets, flutes, fifes, or other musical instruments, or for the shooting off of a "great peale of ordinaunce" (*Jocasta*); sometimes, for a particular music—a "dead march [to be] plaid" during the pantomime (*Tancred and Gismund*). Whether the silent action is introduced or accompanied by "gastly fearefull chimes of night" that "with a dolefull peale [fill] the roofe with sounds of tragedie" (*A Warning for Fair Women*) or "louder musicke . . . To yeeld, as fits the act, a Tragicke sound" (*The White Devil*) or the discharging of "peeces" that with the sounds of "drommes and fluites" and the marching of armed men signify "tumults, rebellions, armes and ciuill warres" (*Gorboduc*), or whether the sounds carry no particular symbolic signification, noise of some kind is a conventional element of the dumb show. Shakespeare employs this convention: the sound of trumpets (or, in the First Folio, of hautboys) introduces his silent scene. But given throughout the play figurative links between noise and evil; a line in the dialogue linking noise with dumb shows; the *chainlike*, noisy ritual of the sound of drum, trumpet, and cannon in a play where one form of "dumb show" leads to another and one "show of violence" to another; a frequent figurative identification of both noise and dumbness with implements of destruction (as we shall see in a study of the figurative patterns) —one is led to suspect that Shakespeare is exploiting the fact that he has an audience conditioned to connecting noise with dumb show and to equating that noise with disorder and tragedy. It would follow that the story of the Ghost, the dumb show, and *Gonzago* are not only all "dumb show"; all, including the dumb show proper, are also a matter of "noise."

The content of the shows elsewhere in English drama is variable in nature. But certain subjects recur: we have observed that one form of the show often presents a company of mourners or a funeral procession; another is the representation of a murder, especially one that is horrible, strange, ingenious (see, for example, *The Battle of Alcazar* or *The White Devil*).[8] A matter of physical unreality—of the magical or the supernatural—is also common to the show. And in plays that, generally speaking, appear after *Hamlet*, the mute scene is used to display false appearance, artificiality, hollowness. In such cases, the dumb show becomes a means for presenting "show," and the dramatist thus evokes metaphorical equations between technique and content. Dieter Mehl points to this development; and, in relation to the thesis of the present study, his observations are so pertinent that I quote them in some detail. Speaking of Marston's use in *Antonio and Mellida* of a silent scene on the main stage while eavesdroppers in the gallery comment on it, he says that a remark by Mellida, one of the onlookers, makes it "clear that for her [the pantomime] was only an empty show"; on *The Revenger's Tragedy*, "We find recurring references to masques, revels, and other courtly entertainments as particularly sinister manifestations of the depravity of the rich. It is only fitting in this play that the installation of the profligate Lussurioso as Duke should be presented as a dumb show. It is a hollow triumph, full of outward 'show,' but doomed from the beginning"; on *Women Beware Women*, "Within the main plot complications arise chiefly out of the contrast between the simple conditions in the house of Leantio and the splendid world of the Court. . . . While the special atmosphere in Leantio's house is conveyed by means of the language, by dialogue and description, the world of the Court is presented by magnificent 'show' "; and Mehl adds that the way in which "Bianca is attracted by the deceptive lustre of the court" (which is presented in dumb show) is "underlined by the deliberate choice of artistic means." Of the dumb show in *The Changeling*, he says, "Such a mode of presentation implies some oblique comment."[9]

In short, Mehl finds the substance of these dumb shows peculiarly attuned to the nature of the device. Similarly, though the dumb show in *Hamlet* presents the conventional ingenious murder, though there is nothing unusual in the choice of content, all signs point to the conclusion that its presentation in dumb show invests that matter with a particular significance. But before continuing with this aspect of Shakespeare's manipulation of the convention, let us turn for the moment to obvious differences between the dumb show in *Hamlet* and other mimes, differences sometimes cited as evidence that Shakespeare's dumb show is unique.

We have seen that far from dispensing with common components of the pantomime, Shakespeare emphasizes them: he makes use of the familiar elements of noise and repetition, and he employs a familiar form and a familiar subject matter. Mere differences between his show and those in other plays are not necessarily relevant to the question of "uniqueness." A study of the history of the convention reveals, for example, considerable variation in the positioning of the pantomime, in its importance, and in the use of accompanying interpretative comment: the dumb show may appear before or between acts, or as a scene within an act; it may appear alone, or in juxtaposition with a dialogue scene; it may be superfluous to the plot or an organic part of it; it may or may not be a part of a prologue; it may include an explanatory narrative, provided by a chorus or a presenter, who may be either outside or inside the action of the play proper. And the pantomime adapts to a great variety of uses: it may be employed to telescope history; to accommodate large sections of plot; to explain the dramatic situation; to foreshadow coming events, prefiguring tragedy; to furnish didactic comment on the following scene or the whole drama; to provide an entertaining interlude; or to serve any of a number of other purposes. In short, the fact that the show in *Hamlet* is not necessary to the plot (or that prologue, presenter, and accompanying interpretative observations do not reflect a hard-and-fast rule) does not—as some critics appear to suggest—establish its singularity. The device is so versatile that the exceptional nature of the *Hamlet* mime cannot be defined by saying that it does not do what pantomime elsewhere may do, especially when shows elsewhere may be directed toward ends obviously irrelevant to Shakespeare's needs.

What is perhaps more to the point is the frequent observation that the show is extraordinary in that it lacks the figurative disguise often found in pantomimes with which it appears to have some elements in common. Mehl observes that there are "many plays where the content of the dumb show is repeated in the dialogue" but that "in all these the dumb show is allegorical or symbolic and does not exactly anticipate the particular plot of the play"; and he adds that in *Hamlet* "dumb show and play [being] themselves parts of a very complex drama" an allegorical pantomime here "might have detracted too much from the actual play and puzzled the spectators unnecessarily."[10] But the dumb show in *Hamlet* may lack a familiar allegorical form and still not lack a figurative disguise. Shakespeare's technique here is one that remarkably accommodates two audiences. If he had used his dumb-show characters in a conventional allegorical or symbolic fashion, his moral comment would tend to be confined, pointed at the play-within-the-play and at the stage audience (as it would be if he had used a conventional presenter). And if he wants the mime to contain comment on *Hamlet* as well as *Gonzago* and to be directed at the *Hamlet* audience as well as the *Gonzago* audience, he has a problem quite different from that of the playwright whose dumb show precedes a section of the play proper and is intended for the edification of the off-stage audience or who aims a symbolic comment at an audience within the play.[11]

I propose that in *Hamlet* the show *is* used for symbolic ends. Early and late, the mime appears in plays on a "Senecan" mode; it is particularly identified with such tragedies[12] and, attached to them, almost invariably presents an action of violence, grief, disruption of order, of unnaturalness and "noise." I propose that Shakespeare evokes the ideas in this ready-made symbolism; that he makes an imaginative leap from a familiar matter of the dumb show to "dumb show" as a definition of that matter; that he defines evil and unreality as "dumb show";[13] and that his extraordinary manipulation of the ordinary elements of the pantomime reinforces a complex figurative comment on two alternatives for "action" on the world stage: the *seeming* that makes life a "dumb show" and the *being* that makes it true play, a mirroring of Nature.

A habit of mind that can produce such figurative equivalences is characteristic of Shakespeare. And these particular connections are not unique in seventeenth-century thought: Thomas Browne, for example, is later to define "dumbe showes" as lacking in "reality, truth, or constancy."[14] Moreover, as we have observed, other playwrights identify unreality, falsehood, and instability by presenting them in dumb show. There is nothing far-fetched in an equation of "dumb show" and evil: the history of the convention promotes it. There is nothing far-fetched in an equation of "dumb show" and unreality: again, conventional practices foreshadow such a connection. Pantomime, as we have remarked, is not uncommonly used to represent a dream or a vision,[15] or to project the imaginings of a character on the stage. Moreover, Mehl notes that "in the earlier classical tragedies the pantomimes help to remove the play even further from reality than it would be without them. By the symbolic interpretation of the action through the pantomimes . . . the spectator is continually reminded of the unreal character of the performance."[16] The traditional practice of providing by way of the silent scene a change in the level of dramatic reality, as well as the traditional employment of magic and the supernatural in dumb show and its use to represent dream and vision, makes it an easy step to identifying "dumb show" with unreality. And the connection traditionally drawn between unreality and evil further elucidates Shakespeare's use of the dumb show.

Critics sometimes point to Ophelia's surmise that the show "imports the argument of the play" (III.ii.150). Dover Wilson, saying that "there appears to be no other example in Elizabethan drama of a dumb-show setting forth an argument,"[17] finds its uniqueness in this use. But Mehl observes that Ophelia's use of the "word argument . . . could as well apply to an allegorical presentation of the plot" of *Gonzago* as to its "exact plot."[18] Both Wilson and Mehl (like Ophelia) refer to the argument of the play-within-the-play, although both (unlike Ophelia) have the "import" of another play to consider. And whether the word refers literally or figuratively to *Gonzago* or whether there are arguments in other dumb shows, Ophelia's remark is indeed suggestive and Shakespeare's method indeed unique: by investing the dumb show with symbolic meaning, he uses it to import the argument of the play, but of *Hamlet*, as well as *Gonzago*.

We have seen that the echoes of familiar forms and components of the dumb show suggest that from the time when the Ghost of the dead King (dumb to the watch and to Horatio) strikes the onlookers dumb or elicits from them "the show of violence," to the end of the play when the violent show of general death also strikes the watchers dumb, "mutes . . . to this act," the matter of the dumb show sounds through the play; that, like the reverberations of "earthly thunder," dumb shows and noise echo dumb shows and noise; that the "act" that "thunders in the index" (III.iv.51–52) still thunders in the dumb epilogue as the noise of the ordnance marks the funeral procession preceding a promised "show" where the "bodies / High on a stage [will] be placed to the view" (V.ii. 388–89) and Horatio—who first tells Hamlet about the "form of the thing" (I.ii.210)—plans to play the presenter telling the "unknowing world / How these things came about" (V. ii.390–91). The sequence that begins with the pouring of poison into a man's ear ends with Hamlet's last words, "The rest is silence" (369); with a description of Claudius, "The ears are senseless that should give us hearing" (380); and with the promise of a silent tableau with declamatory accompaniment. In short, the dumb show proper—a mime of murder and a "show of violence"—presents the argument of *Hamlet*, which contains a chain of silent scenes and pantomimic actions, all instinct with death. Nevertheless, the distinction between *Hamlet* and the court entertainment—the dumb show and *Gonzago*—is part of that argument; nor should the form and content of Horatio's proposed "show" and presentation be identified, as it sometimes is in critical writing, with the form and content of *Hamlet*. For we shall see that Shakespeare distinguishes between seeming and reality by way of these instances of "show."

In Shakespeare's hands, the dumb show is not only a piece of stagecraft centrally placed in the structure of the drama; it is also a definition central to comment on the action that makes life a hollow show and the antithetical action that gives substance to a performance on the world stage. In other plays, the dumb show may serve to define, in a limited context, vanity and pomp and self-serving; beastliness and depravity; artificiality, false-seeming, unreality, and emptiness; the isolation and circumscription attendant on evil. But in *Hamlet*, "dumb

31

show" becomes an extended metaphor, and elements of the dumb show—repetition, noise accompaniment, form, and content—implement an essential symbolic commentary. Exactly what "dumb show" represents and exactly what it leads to is developed in a figurative design grounded in the facts of the Ghost's story. The poison-ear imagery, the confinement and the beast-trap imagery, which we shall now explore, take their point from the literal details of the murder of King Hamlet, details that lead to the presentation of the dumb show and are recapitulated in it. Thus, a figurative pattern based on the particulars of a murder explicates the nature, operation, and effect of "show" in general and of "show" in *Hamlet* in particular. We shall see that the burden of the figurative design picks up the burden of the pantomimic action that echoes through the play like a refrain and choruses the movement of Hamlet's tragedy: "a-down a-down . . . a-down-a. O, how the wheel becomes it!" sings Ophelia in madness (IV.v.170–72). And the way in which Shakespeare here fuses technique and meaning—so that the wheel, the refrain, recalls the descriptions of Fortune's wheel "bowl[ing] . . . down the hill of heaven, / As low as to the fiends" and of the "cease of majesty . . . a massy wheel"—is the way in which he uses the dumb show to define "dumb show."

CHAPTER THREE

I

The event that marks the overt genesis of the tragedy is violence in a garden. And the rehearsal of this act first in description, then in pantomime, and then once again in dramatic action with dialogue, serves to underscore its particulars. That it takes place in a garden, that the destroyer is envious and treacherous, that he wishes to usurp the place of another, that he is called a "serpent" (I.v.39), that he attacks by way of the ears, that the immediate effect of his evildoing is a species of confinement for the victim (a "loathsome crust," [72])—these details, even the information that royalty is sleeping, echo the first act of treachery in a garden, its circumstances, cause, and effect. And this echo, to be repeatedly reinforced in metaphor, as well as in the general ruin that follows on Claudius's deed, helps to place the *Hamlet* story in a universal context. Such allusions as those connecting Claudius with Satan (and Cain) bear on what Shakespeare ultimately defines as "dumb show" and are part of a recurrent comment on a natural inheritance that compounds man's difficulties in making existence something other than mere "show."

But in exploring the meaning in the complex figurative design based on the literal details of King Hamlet's death, it will prove most expedient to separate the strands of the pattern and, so far as possible, to observe separately the implications in each. We shall focus first on the *method* of the murder, on the figurative use made of it, and on Shakespeare's purpose in keeping constantly before us not just the fact of the slaying but the peculiar physical means by which it is accomplished. It has been observed that though ingenious murders are a commonplace in the literature of the time, the method described in *Hamlet* is unusual[1] and, less frequently, that its special oddity lies in the poison's being introduced into *both* ears of the sleeper.[2] But that this fact informs a profusion of figurative references to "ears" and attack by way of them has not received the attention it merits.[3]

Bernardo's account to Horatio of the previous appearances of the Ghost is introduced by the words, "Let us once again assail your ears" (I.i.31). When these words are spoken, at the very opening of the play, no details of King Hamlet's death have been given; and the picture evoked by a phrasing not uncommon in Shakespeare's plays does not particularly catch one's attention. But this line strikes a note that is to become a leitmotif in the play; and a subsequent figurative interplay that links speech with poison and repeatedly recalls that King Hamlet's death came as a result of having poison poured into his ears, supports the proposition, in retrospect, that Bernardo's words may be a vial of "cursed hebenon," a poison with which he, however innocently, "assails" the ears of his hearers. Horatio, in turn, is to repeat the figure, though less suggestively, at the beginning of *his* account to Hamlet of the Ghost's appearance: "Season your admiration for a while / With an attent ear" (I.ii.192–93). If such echoes were isolated or infrequent (or all like this last one, a commonplace turn of the phrase), they would be inconsequential. But again and again Shakespeare is to emphasize the idea that attack, infection, destruction, can come by way of the ears, not only in the form of a literal poison, but in the form of *noise*, of words that cleave, stab, shoot, or carry plague: Hamlet speaks of "cleav[ing] the general ear with horrid speech" (II.ii.589); Gertrude says, "These words, like daggers, enter in mine ears" (III.iv.95); Laertes "wants not buzzers to infect his ear / With pestilent speeches of his father's death" (IV.v.90–91); Claudius says,

"This [arraigning 'in ear and ear'] / Like to a murdering-piece, in many places / Gives me superfluous death" (94–96).

Given the literal particulars of King Hamlet's murder, such figurative language is most evocative; reminders of the character of the original crime are thus perpetuated in lines that suggest an approximate means and method of destruction. A pointed link between "abuse" by hebenon and by speech is made in the story of the Ghost: after Claudius pours the poison into his brother's ears, he resorts to what both metaphor and circumstance suggest is another kind of poison, and "the whole ear of Denmark / Is by a forged process of [the King's] death / Rankly abused" (I.v.36–38). Thus, poison and speech are connected by the poisoner's attack on the ear of Denmark, first by hebenon and then by false report, as well as by the identification elsewhere of both with murderous weaponry and the description of the operation of both in an imagery of infection. Sometimes Shakespeare rather simply and explicitly links speech and poison: in the First Player's Speech, we are told that anyone who had seen Hecuba's grief "with tongue in venom steep'd, / . . . would treason have pronounced" (II.ii.533–34), and Hamlet calls a certain speech "Wormwood" (III.ii.191). But usually the connection is made by implicit equivalents between speech and poison, disease, weapons, or the sound of guns. Not infrequently, several of these are interacting components in one metaphorical statement: for example, a "whisper o'er the world's diameter, / As level as the cannon to his blank, / Transports his poison'd shot" (IV.i.41–43). And when words are thus repeatedly identified with poison in a play where a man is killed by having a "leperous distilment" (I.v.64) poured into his ears, the implication in Bernardo's "Let us once again assail your ears" that the "story" of the Ghost's appearance may be a poison cannot be discounted, and the reiterated suggestion that infection may lie in "pestilent speeches" about a "father's death" cannot be ignored.

Moreover, the idea that hebenon is not the only harmful substance that can be introduced into ears is repeated insistently. Early in the play when Hamlet asks Horatio, "What, in faith, make you from Wittenburg?" and Horatio answers, "A truant disposition," Hamlet responds, "I would not hear your enemy say so, / Nor shall you do mine ear that violence, / To make it truster of your own report / Against yourself" (I.ii.168–73). On the surface, this is mere playful, courteous exchange; but Hamlet's words take on weight from a pattern in which they are one detail and from their bearing on subsequent repetitions of the image and subsequent event. As in other instances mentioned above, "report" is here described as something that may "do [the] ear . . . violence"; and however inconsequent the context, there is the additional implication, a most significant one in view of immediate developments in action, that trust in the speaker provides protection against "that violence." Then in the scene immediately following, Laertes declares that "best safety lies in fear" (I.iii.43) and, admonishing Ophelia to hold Hamlet's avowals of love "a toy in blood" (6), tells her, "Weigh what loss your honour may sustain, / If with too credent ear you list" (29–30). Thus— in words couched in the same ear/speech imagery—Laertes repeats Hamlet's remark that one must not always believe what one hears, but he repeats it with a difference: protection from the violence in speech lies in fear, not in trust. There is, no doubt, a practical wisdom in what Laertes says; but Shakespeare underscores the idea that the "sleeping" ear may invite disaster, not only by again having a character say as much, but by having him say so in a context where his own advice is dangerous to the well-being of the hearer. It occurs neither to Ophelia nor to Laertes that she might well apply his warning to his own words. And the irony is compounded when, shortly after she agrees not to listen with "too credent ear" and thus to guard her honor, she listens to Polonius and submits to his opinion of what "behoves [his] daughter and [her] honour." There is further irony and further play on the same metaphor when Polonius advises Laertes, "Give every man thy ear, but few thy voice" (68). Again this sounds like a good practical precept; but Polonius is, very shortly, to charge his daughter not to "so slander any moment leisure, / As to give words or talk with the Lord Hamlet" (133–34). His son, in adopting a conduct that ensures his not being "false to any man," must have an open ear; his daughter, in the name of honor, must close her ears.

In the large context of death-by-poison-administered-through-the-ears, Shakespeare gets a lot of mileage from these speech/ear images. On the one hand, they provide a kaleidoscopic commentary on the characters and action within the scenes marked by an imagery that perpetuates a connection between words and hebenon. Polonius, earlier the moralizer and advocate of truth to all men, is to tell Reynaldo, when he soon after sends him to spy on Laertes, "Put on him [Laertes] / What forgeries you please" (II.i.19–20), an instruction that follows the scene where the Ghost connects a "forged process" with "abuse." When Polonius is thus false to his son and indirectly abusive, albeit he intends to act in Laertes' best interests, one is led to reconsider not just the irony in Laertes' giving ear to such a father's preachments but the practical wisdom in "Give every man thy ear, but few thy voice," if (with men like Polonius around) this may entail giving ear to "forgeries," an act that in turn (according to Polonius's words to Reynaldo), is followed by the hearer's "giv[ing] voice" to corroboration of that slander.

The self-contradictions in Polonius's speech, the inconsistency in his charges to Laertes and Ophelia, his hasty assumption that Hamlet's vows are false and his consequent charge to Ophelia (just after he has sermonized on being open-minded and on giving "thoughts no tongue, / Nor any unproportion'd thought his act" [I.iii.59–60]), must lead one to reflect on the ambivalent nature of the trust that Hamlet says is a means of holding off the violence in speech. Not only does Ophelia's trust in her father ironically demonstrate the truth in both Hamlet's and Laertes' claim that one must not always credit what one hears; it even more ironically reveals the rub in both Laertes' philosophy that safety lies in fear and Hamlet's that it lies in trust, since Ophelia chooses the wrong objects for fear and trust: that is, whether or not she, in fact, fears Hamlet's "holy vows" (114) and trusts to her father's interpretation of them, she *acts* on those premises. And Shakespeare comments further on the problem when two faiths or allegiances are at odds by having Hamlet contradict, in action, his own words. His protestation of such a trust in Horatio that he will not believe Horatio's self-accusation may occur in a trivial context; but it is put to a test in a situation that is not trivial. And after the words of the Ghost have entered Hamlet's ears, Horatio's assurance that he will not make known what he has seen, his declaring by his "faith" that he will not, are not guarantee enough for Hamlet. Despite his earlier protest, he insists that Horatio "swear by [the] sword," a phrase repeated five times and implied by the word "swear" as many times again. The "sword" supplants the "faith" that both Horatio and Marcellus invoke in their reluctance to swear; yet the sword itself represents a faith, one embraced by the Ghost, who repeatedly echoes Hamlet's word "swear" (I.v.145–81).

While the interplay of fact and figure spotlights particular circumstance (when expressed rules of conduct are contradicted in action by their exponents or are shown to require a qualification not envisaged by the speaker), it also illuminates the larger dramatic action. The postulates that speech may be an agent for violence; that faith (or fear) may serve as a bulwark against the harm in speech only insofar as it is not misplaced; that a speaker may, by a failure in character or understanding, be an unwitting purveyor of harm to those whose welfare he has at heart; that two faiths may be antithetic (since Ophelia's giving "too credent ear" to her father's charge adds up to closing her ears to what she considers "holy vows of heaven"); that neither the open nor the closed ear is automatically invulnerable, but rather that one's well-being depends on what one chooses to act on—all are relevant to the large movement of the play. Since such ideas are stressed in passages immediately preceding and immediately following Hamlet's encounter with the Ghost, they must be taken into account in considering the import of that meeting. In the scene where the Ghost informs Hamlet of the literal poisoning-by-way-of-the-ears, Shakespeare has the speaker repeatedly enjoin the hearer to listen ("Lend thy serious hearing," "List, list, O, list," "Now, Hamlet, hear" [I.v.5,22,34]); he not only stresses "hearing" but points to a violent effect of it ("I am bound to hear," says Hamlet; and the Ghost replies, "So art thou to revenge, when thou shalt hear"). The Ghost's insistence on his son's *listening* to his story and its burden of revenge in the name of love and honor, just after another father, also in the name of honor, tells his son to open his ears to all men and his daughter to close hers, and just before that other father's concept of honor is shown to be as limited as his instructions are contradictory, must take on a significance from the emphasis in the juxtaposed scenes on the potentially destructive nature of speech. Despite all the obvious differences in character, circumstance, and command, the two fathers reflect similar attitudes: both are concerned with family honor; both exhibit self-regard; and both define a relationship between another man and a woman as a matter of lust. The fact that Shakespeare reveals Polonius as a cynical, conceited, self-contradictory, deceitful schemer (however well-intentioned) does not, of course, justify our transferring some such criticism to the Ghost, simply because the scenes in which the two fathers address their offspring are joined and because Polonius and the Ghost display some of the same views. But the whole force of the figurative pattern and the manipulation of situation and incident demand that the Ghost's charge, like Polonius's instructions, be viewed in relation to the danger in "giving ear."

Another cluster of figures reinforces the suggestion. Laertes rephrases his warning against the loss that may follow on listening with "too credent ear" by cautioning Ophelia against "contagious blastments" (I.iii.42). Thus, *contagion* and *blastments* are identified with speech or the effect of speech. That talk can take on the property of poison is again implied by the use of forms of the words *blast* to describe both. Hamlet calls the poisoning of King Hamlet a "blasting" (III.iv.65), and the Ghost's description of the "tetter" that "bark'd about" his body supports the connotation of blight in the word; elsewhere, we have noted the reference to Hecate's curse that "thrice blasted, thrice infected" the mixture Lucianus pours into Gonzago's ears: both "cursed hebenon" and cursed speech can blast and infect. The associations of disease in the word *blast* are picked up when Laertes uses "blastments" in connection with the "canker" that galls the bud (I.iii.39–42) and when Hamlet uses "blasting" to describe the act of the "mildew'd ear" Claudius (III.iv.64); and such associations are reiterated in phrases like "this canker of our nature" (V.ii.69), which Hamlet calls the king who "blast[s] his wholesome brother." The figurative comment on disease and decay that extends the motif of poisoning has been discussed in a number of critical papers; but the connection afforded in forms of the word *blast* between speech (or noise) and disease or poison has been generally neglected.[4]

What particularly concerns us here, however, is not just the demonstrable link between speech and poison and between both and a "blasting" but also, given such equivalences, the connection between the appearances of the Ghost and "blastments." Besides connoting the disease found elsewhere in the speech images, *blast* denotes gusts of wind and cold. Laertes' use of "contagious blastments" evokes the weather, as well as the "canker" that galls "the infants of the spring." And his warning follows shortly on the Ghost's appearance before the watch on a night of "bitter cold" and "sick[ness] at heart" (I.i.8–9), when an explicit connection is drawn between the Ghost and potential blast: Horatio determines to speak to the Ghost "though it blast [him]" (127). Thus, the weather that marks his next coming ("The air bites shrewdly; it is very cold"), the *blast* of trumpets that precedes it, the reiteration of the word ("Bring with thee airs from heaven or blasts from hell, . . . I will speak to thee," says Hamlet, [I.iv.41,44]) suggest, in more ways than one, a climate of "contagious blastments," not of heavenly "airs."

This is not yet to arrive at any flat conclusions about the character of the Ghost and his mission; it is to insist that the method and the means of the murder that propels the tragedy are neither casual details nor a mere pandering to a popular taste for the strange and the sensational, but rather a carefully contrived base for a study of the contamination in evil, its chain-reaction, and the various forms it takes—even, for example, a "show" of good. There is simply no doubt that the speech/ear figures repeatedly say that as hebenon "blasted" the wholesome blood, so speech may contaminate, that as poison brought on a "leperous" death, so words may infect and destroy; no doubt that both poison and cursed speech are equated with "blasting" and "contagion"; no doubt that the Ghost's appearance is connected with blastments and sickness-at-heart, that blastments and contagion are linked with "too credent ear," and that the Ghost insists on Hamlet's "serious hearing." The movement of the pattern, whatever qualifications one may advance, leads to the possibility that the Ghost, although he eschews an "eternal blazon . . . To ears of flesh and blood" (I.v.21–22) and would not have his son's mind tainted, does "do [Hamlet's] ear . . . violence" and that the original method and means of murder informs an ironic but logical process wherein a poisoned man's speech becomes a potential poison and a victim a latent poisoner.

II

The chain-reaction of evil is one of the motifs of the whole dramatic action; and we have seen that the speech/ear imagery carries several strains of this burden. What affects the King affects Denmark; this point is reinforced, the pestilential nature of evil demonstrated, by the figurative account of Claudius's pouring poison into the whole ear of Denmark to consolidate the gains of poisoning a king. The accompanying proposition in the metaphor, that one wrong deed breeds another in the doer, reappears in subsequent action, most pointedly when killing a nephew becomes, in Claudius's diseased mind, a justifiable sequel to killing a brother. But that the wrong done an individual may spread to the general and that the transgressor is likely to sin again are not the only refrains of the figurative comment on the burgeoning of evil. Another particular of the contagion in wrongdoing is that an evil act by one man may elicit like action in another. In various ways, Shakespeare implies that the ear that is poisoned becomes itself a poisoner: if Claudius "like a mildew'd ear, / Blast[s] his wholesome brother," then the logical inference extends beyond the mere fact of destruction, to the implication that Hamlet Senior becomes a mildewed ear.

It may be argued that to read thus is to read too precisely; obviously, Hamlet, who employs the phrase, has no such thought in mind. But it is unlikely that Shakespeare does not invite a reading that he continually supports. The Ghost appears just after Hamlet speaks to Horatio of the "dram of eale" that corrupts "all the noble substance":

> So, oft it chances in particular men,
> That for some vicious mole of nature in them,
> As, in their birth—wherein they are not guilty,
> Since nature cannot choose his origin—
> By the o'ergrowth of some complexion,
> Oft breaking down the pales and forts of reason,
> Or by some habit that too much o'er-leavens
> The form of plausive manners, that these men
> Carrying, I say, the stamp of one defect,
> Being nature's livery, or fortune's star,—
> Their virtues else—be they as pure as grace,
> As infinite as man may undergo—
> Shall in the general censure take corruption
> From that particular fault: the dram of eale
> Doth all the noble substance of a doubt
> To his own scandal.
>
> (I.iv.23–28)

These words are hardly out of Hamlet's mouth when the Ghost appears.[5] Comment on a newcomer by way of a speech just preceding his entrance or on a dramatic situation by way of the dialogue just prior to it is a technique not uncommonly employed by Shakespeare. Certainly, the matter that the Ghost relates concerns a dram of evil:

> Upon my secure hour thy uncle stole,
> With juice of cursed hebenon in a vial,
> And in the porches of my ears did pour
> The leperous distilment: whose effect
> Holds such an enmity with blood of man
> That swift as quicksilver it courses through
> The natural gates and alleys of the body,
> And with a sudden vigour it doth posset
> And curd, like eager droppings into milk,
> The thin and wholesome blood: so did it mine;

44

And a most instant tetter bark'd about,
Most lazar-like, with vile and loathsome crust,
All my smooth body.

(I.v.61–73)

Though Claudius's "drain[ing] his draughts of Rhenish" initiates Hamlet's speech to Horatio, *dram* denotes a small amount, as a vial contains a small portion. It is surely not accident that Shakespeare should juxtapose references to a noxious dram and to a vial, the contents of which are "leperous." And in defining the "one defect" equated with the "dram of eale," Hamlet has named "some vicious mole of nature in [men], / As, in their birth." Again, it is surely not coincidence that a reference to a "mole of nature"—a figure that evokes faults in the blood: a specific family inheritance, as well as a general human inheritance—should immediately precede a scene where a father's Ghost is called an "old mole" (I.v.162).[6] The play of fancy between the passage where Hamlet philosophizes on the one defect, "nature's livery, or fortune's star," from which "particular men" take corruption and the dialogue and circumstance in the following scene is remarkably rich; yet it is consistently in line with the logic of the comment in the ear/speech imagery. The appearance of the Ghost on the heels of a speech about a contaminating "mole" or "dram," joined to his vivid description of the literal effect a dram of poison had on him, to the demonstration of its abstract effect in the injunction to revenge, and then to his being called a "mole," is part of the pattern suggesting that Hamlet Senior has been infected in more than physical ways by the evil done him, that his noble substance has become a destructive essence, and that the words he urges on Hamlet's hearing represent another form of hebenon.

Repetitions and metaphorical equivalences reiterated in different ways cannot be dismissed as mere chance. It is a constant of the figurative pattern that the man who is poisoned is described as both poisoner and poisonous substance. Claudius, poisoned by ambition and passion, becomes not only a poisoner, but a "canker." And Hamlet Senior, poisoned literally, becomes a "mole." This echo of the phrase "the mole of nature," which Hamlet calls the defect that breaks down the "forts of reason," and Hamlet's adoption of the action of madness after listening to the "old mole" imply that the Ghost has taken corruption from both "this canker of our nature" Claudius and the old defect in man's nature; that he, like Claudius, is a defect; and that he, like Claudius, is a transmitter of defect. The logical continuation of such a process is manifest in Claudius's description of Hamlet in words that recall the working of the poison in the blood of Hamlet Senior: "like the hectic in my blood he rages" (IV.iii.68). That one man's evil act may elicit like action in another man is a principle of the design that shows the mildewed ear blasting his brother, who in turn blasts his son, who in turn becomes a blaster. And the figurative link between Hamlet's effect on Claudius and the effect of the poison on Hamlet Senior also contains the principle that evil recoils on the evil-doer.

Both of these themes are graphically and brilliantly illustrated by the chain of noise that sounds and resounds in the first and the last acts of the play and thus provides a frame for a whole action that Horatio is eventually to sum up in the phrase, "purposes . . . Fall'n on the inventors' heads" (V.ii.395–96). We have seen that equivalences are drawn between speech and weaponry and that the operation of both is delineated in an imagery of contagion. In the descriptions of the chain of noise initiated by Claudius's "rouse," Shakespeare turns the perspective around and instead of defining speech as dagger, cannon, "murdering-piece," he describes the use and sound of the paraphernalia of battle—kettles, trumpets, and cannon—as speech. In the first act when Claudius drinks to "jocund health," he says that each time he drinks a "pledge," the cannon will "tell" it to the clouds and "the king's rouse the heaven shall bruit again, / Re-speaking earthly thunder" (I.ii.125–28); in the last act when he drinks to Hamlet's "better breath," he says, "Let all the battlements their ordnance fire, / . . . And let the kettle to the trumpet speak, / The trumpet to the cannoneer without, / The cannons to the heavens, the heavens to earth, / 'Now the king drinks to Hamlet' " (V.ii.281,286–89). Thus drums and trumpets "bray" a "pledge" (I.iv.11–12) and "speak"; cannons "tell" and

"speak"; and the emphasis is on the echoing and the reechoing of this particular "speaking," a detail enriched by connotations of counting in the word "tell" and of rumor, echo,
and clamor in the word "bruit." Elsewhere, we have seen
Shakespeare repeatedly point to the violence inherent in
speech; here he describes sounds familiar to the battlefield
as speech. Elsewhere, he says that cursed speech may spread
infection; here he describes a sequence where the "speaking"
of one weapon or martial sound is echoed by another.

On both occasions, the military noise marks a social custom
and is itself a customary ritual. On both occasions, the practice is revealed as something other than the ceremonious pledge
of faith, honor, and health that it is supposed to be. Of the
first instance, Hamlet says, "It is a custom / More honour'd
in the breach than the observance" (I.iv.15–16); and he moves
from a criticism of a specific fault that soils reputation to a
general comment on the corrupting *dram*, any fault that may
poison the whole nature.[7] The declaration of such a large consequence (in a passage containing a subtle reminder that it
was an example of intemperance in drink that led to the statement) is especially significant in a play where one man's inordinate ambition and love lead him to capital sins against
order and pollute a nature in which there are still glimpses
of original worth and where another man is given occasion
for inordinate anger and grief. Moreover, Hamlet's questioning
of the honor in a social custom is most suggestive, since he is
shortly to be faced with the premise that he can attest to
his honor only by observing an aristocratic ideal of revenge.
But what particularly concerns us now about the two occasions marked by the shooting-off of the ordnance is the play
of figure and fact that defines the custom and thus the noise
that reflects it. The initial ceremony is described by Hamlet
in a speech that links it with a "complexion," a "habit," a
"particular fault." The "heavy-headed revel" leads him to reflect on the "dram of eale," a phrase that picks up the motif
of poisoning since, like the vial of hebenon that "posset[s]"
the "wholesome blood," the dram of eale brings corruption to
the "noble substance." Thus, the metaphorical relationships
suggest that what Claudius views as a celebration of "jocund

47

health" is, in fact, a kind of ritualistic poisoning.[8] And the implication that appearance and reality are at odds, that what the noise symbolizes is not health or honor or admirable custom but a poisoning of sorts, is clinched on the second occasion when Claudius, saying, "Give me drink. Hamlet, this pearl is thine; / Here's to thy health" (V.ii.293–94), awards him the "union" in the cup where wine and poison are now literally joined.[9]

The ordnance echoes this act and dignifies it, just as the sound of drum, trumpet, and cannon had imaged the King's "rouse" and glorified a matter of excess. So the noise symbolizes both the ugly nature of the act it celebrates and the fair appearance, the false report, by which evil is often perpetrated. The "forged process" with which Claudius abuses "the whole ear of Denmark" and misrepresents the facts of King Hamlet's death; the "forgeries" that Polonius, in the name of truth, tells Reynaldo to put on Laertes; the false charge that Claudius calls "our sovereign process" when, in the name of love, he commands England to "cure" him (IV.iii.65,69); the resultant forged letter, the "fair" writing of which Hamlet describes in five lines of comment as he tells Horatio how he once held it a "baseness" to write fair (V.ii.32–36); the various false speeches in the play that take the shape of wit, wisdom, morality, authority—all are characterized by this military "speaking" that presents disorder in the guise of order and dignity. In short, the sounds of the ordnance invest ugliness with a fair face and thus, particularly since they are equated with speech, suggest the misleading form a wrong act or speech may assume. Noise symbolizes "show," both pomp and falsehood: what purports to be a celebration of honor is, in fact, one of intemperance, and later a seeming ceremony of kingly faith is, in reality, a matter of treachery.

Second, the sequence of this noise demonstrates the idea noted elsewhere in the speech imagery that the wrong word or act produces a chain of like words and actions. It is particularly fitting in this play that the Danes' drinking custom should initiate echo and reverberation, and that the report of the guns should be identified with speech and a "Re-speaking": the censure in "other nations" occasioned by the Danes' drinking habits is no less false report than the military sounds in Denmark that glorify the habit. The latter call the fault a virtue; but the former, which calls a Dane a swine on the basis of "particular fault," is also a misrepresentation of the truth. Thus, Shakespeare invests the "speaking" of the ordnance with one set of figurative associations by the very nature of the act it celebrates, and with another when Hamlet explains to Horatio the echoing sounds that follow on the King's draining "his draughts of Rhenish" and then alludes to the talk in other nations that also follows on such revel. The latent analogy throws suspicion on the talk that "soil[s the Danes'] addition" (I.iv.20): if excess evokes the "swinish phrase" (19), the latter is itself open to censure since it is excessive and, masquerading as righteous moral judgment, presents a half-truth as a whole truth. And Shakespeare thus extends his comment on the ambivalent forms a wrong-speaking may take and on the chain effect of wrong-doing.

Third, in the descriptions of both drinking ceremonies, the heavens respeak earthly thunder. Such a detail supports one of the basic themes of the play, that evil recoils on the evil-doer. A reverberation from the heavens implies judgment, specifically a consequence that fits the crime; and the boomerang of bad intentions is repeatedly illustrated in the action of the play: one sees, for example, the sinner "hoist with his own petar" when Laertes, poisoned by his own venom, says, "The foul practice / Hath turn'd itself on me" (V.ii.328–29). The end-effect of the chain of sound elucidates the instances of backlash in the dramatic action: the man who sets in motion the sound of evil, whether it embodies a small or a great sin against order, and the man who fails to heed anything but "earthly thunder" are bound to bear its reverberations. Caroline Spurgeon's observations that Shakespeare connects disorder with noise and clamor, that he uses "the peculiar quality of echoing and re-echoing sound . . . to emphasize . . . the incalculable and boundless effects of evil," that he is concerned with "the quickly spreading and infectious quality of evil" and the "reverberations of the evil deed"[10]—all are supported by the use of noise in *Hamlet*.

We have noted the implication that man has the means to

safeguard himself against poison of an immaterial nature, an idea that, as we shall see, is reiterated in another cluster of images. But in this tragedy there are few demonstrations of the argument that the ear may be spiritually proof against the violence potential in word or act. What *is* illustrated in the action is the primary comment in the speech and noise imagery: that words—like firearm, poison, or disease—may blast; that evil may assail the ears in forms that take on a *show* of morality, righteous judgment, admirable custom, sovereign process, the appearance of order, justice, and love; and that such speech, disseminating its evil, inevitably rebounds on the speaker. Repeatedly, the wordplay recalling the facts of the original murder suggests the abuse in speech and the vulnerability of the hearer: "A knavish speech sleeps in a foolish ear," says Hamlet (IV.ii.25–26). Repeatedly, it suggests the contamination that spreads from the "mildew'd ear": "Hark you," Hamlet says to Rosencrantz and Guildenstern, "at each ear a hearer" (II.ii.399–400). The very oddity of this strange phrase recommends it to our attention. At either ear Hamlet places the men whom he later says he will trust as he would "adders fang'd" (III.iv.203) when, as functionaries of the "serpent" Claudius, they bear the "mandate" to England. Yet in the present instance (as in the later) no venom comes from them to Hamlet's ears; he is now (as later) the speaker; and they are the "hearers" of one of his malicious reports on Polonius (as later they will be assailed by his report on themselves in a forgery of a "process," itself a thing of treachery and malice). In "Hark you . . . at each ear a hearer," one catches glimpses of the process revealed elsewhere in the figurative comment: the abused ear turned abuser; victimizers (even unknowing ones) become victims; the contamination in evil, the plague-like lack of distinction in a revenge that "swoopstake . . . will draw both friend and foe." And evoking a background of disaster hidden to Rosencrantz and Guildenstern and not entirely apprehended by Hamlet, the eccentric phrase projects their fate. Like Claudius, they are all subject to the reverberation of their own acts; but like King Hamlet, they are sleeping victims. Unlike Hamlet, Rosencrantz and Guildenstern do not know, until "the great axe fall[s]," that a "sovereign power" may wear only the seeming of justice; but they, too, like Hamlet, are caught in a movement of evil from ear to ear to ear.[11]

The figurative equivalences and connections by which Shakespeare comments on both the murder of King Hamlet and other forms of murder-by-poison-poured-into-the-ears continue throughout the play. At the very end when Claudius lies dead by poisoned weapon and poisoned drink, the First Ambassador, come to tell him that Rosencrantz and Guildenstern are dead, is given evocative and ironic words: "The ears are senseless that should give us hearing . . . Where should we have our thanks?" (V.ii.380, 383). If Claudius had heard this report, he would have found the poison with which he assailed the ear of England returned to his own. As it is, the situation brilliantly recalls Claudius's own earlier description of "pestilent speech" when he said, "[It] gives me superfluous death" (IV.v.96).

The critic who, seeing fault in Hamlet, somehow finds it logical to whitewash Claudius should consider the insistence in the figurative pattern on the mushrooming of evil, once planted, and on the far-reaching and recoiling consequences of the wrong word or act. But those who, seeing Claudius's corruption, therefore find the Ghost's injunction defensible should consider the same pattern. Any conclusion on what Shakespeare says about the nature of the Ghost's mission must take into account an imagery that defines a certain kind of speech by way of the method and the means of a murder—the pouring of a "leperous distilment" into "the porches of [a man's] ears"—and that links a "speaking" with a bad custom; with a noise, a flourish of weaponry which glorifies in a show of honor what is, in fact, a matter of evil.

And any conclusion about the import of the dumb show, which follows on and repeats the Ghost's tale of murder, must take into account not only the idea that speech may have the destructive property of poison or disease or firearm but also the idea that *dumbness* follows on such speech. "I have words to speak in thine ear will make thee dumb; yet are they much too light for the bore of the matter," Hamlet writes to Horatio (IV.vi.24–27). The "matter" is one of murder induced by words, by Claudius's treacherous message to England and Hamlet's treacherous use of it. And the projected tale of that matter is explicated by a language that implicitly identifies the sound of words with the noise of firearms and explicitly forecasts dumbness as the result of an assault on ears, of blasting words. Both noise and dumbness originate in evil, whether drum, trumpet, and cannon "speak" in mere show or tongueless murder "speak[s]" in dumb show (II.ii.622). And whether noise follows on noise in a literal chain of martial sounds; whether dumbness follows on dumbness in a literal chain of pantomimic actions; or whether a "hideous crash" produces a "speechless" silence "as hush as death," which, in turn, leads to "dreadful thunder," the sequela has its "head over [its] shoulder turn'd" (II.i.97). If we consider the implications of a figurative pattern that directs our gaze back to the method and the means of a murder, we can better determine the nature and the purport of a silence begot by dumb show; of a dumb show begot by an injunction to revenge; and of an injunction to revenge begot by murder.

CHAPTER FOUR

I

The immediate literal *effect* of the hebenon is, like the method and the means of the crime, importantly recalled in subsequent image clusters. In vivid detail, the Ghost describes the physical consequence when the "leperous distilment" coursed through the body's "natural gates": "A most instant tetter bark'd about, / Most lazar-like, with vile and loathsome crust, / All my smooth body" (I.v.71–73). Generally, critical comment on the influence of the Ghost's story on the overall figurative design focuses on the leitmotif of poison and its extension in an imagery of disease; on the workings of the actual poison in the blood of the sleeping king and the similar operation of the abstract poison in the body of Denmark;[1] on the process of literal infection resulting from Claudius's murderous act and the descriptions of country and court, subject to Claudius, in an imagery of corruption and rot; on the reappearance of the import of words like "leperous," "lazar-like," "tetter," "crust," "posset," and "curd" in images of festering sores— for example, in "ulcer," "blister," "kibe," "imposthume," "pocky" bodies—and in other expressions that suggest animal or plant decay or both: "canker," "gall," "blast," "blight," "mildew,' and so on. But another figurative pattern growing out of the immediate particular effect of the poison has been neglected: *crust* also informs an imagery of confinement, which develops the theme that an encrustment, an imprisonment, inevitably attends on evil.[2]

Let us first simply list some of the confinement images. Forms of the word *prison* recur, always in connection with an implicit or an explicit account of wrongdoing. The King who dies with "all [his] imperfections on [his] head" (I.v.79) is "doom'd for a certain term" because of "foul crimes" and "confined" during the day to a "prison-house" (10–14). Hamlet cries, "Denmark's a prison" (II.ii.249) after Claudius abuses "the whole ear of Denmark" and the words of the Ghost have entered Hamlet's ears; and he also calls the world a prison with "many confines, wards and dungeons, Denmark being one o' the worst." We have seen a striking instance of Shakespeare's preoccupation with a connection between evil and noise in the passages where "a hideous crash / Takes prisoner Pyrrhus' ear" (498–99), and here again imprisonment is consequent on evil. Aboard the ship bearing Claudius's mandate to England, Hamlet thinks that he lies "worse than the mutines in the bilboes" (V.ii.6). Images of confinement are used to describe both victim and victimizer: not only is the poisoned King "bark'd about"; the poisoner possesses, after the act, a "limed soul" (III.iii.68). The encrusting effect of something damnable is stressed in Hamlet's description of the heart "brass'd" by "damned custom" (III.iv.35–37). The list could be greatly extended: such phrases as "passion's slave" (III.ii.77), putting "fetters" on "fear" (III.iii.25), and the "strict . . . arrest" of the "fell sergeant, death" (V.ii.347–48) develop the motif, as does a cluster of trap images. But if, at present, we can conclude that "prison-house" and "bilboes" and the figurative identification of Denmark, the world, custom, noise, and lime with confinement, establish the presence and variety of the pattern, we have a base for exploring its significance; the comment it affords on the nature and mission of the Ghost; and its relevance to Hamlet's tragedy.

First of all, quite obviously, the "vile crust" is not the result of sin on the part of the one encrusted. And, similarly, any person may be, through no fault of his own, bound by a movement of evil or a whole people caught in a flood set in motion by an individual act of wrongdoing. The idea is an evident theme of the play: one may be the victim of events in which he plays no part, born in a "time [that] is out of joint." And there are lines that stress the limitations put on will and choice by both an individual lot and a general fate: Laertes says of Hamlet, "His will is not his own; / For he himself is subject to his birth" (I.iii.17–18); and we have noted Hamlet's words about "some vicious mole of nature in [men], / As, in their birth—wherein they are not guilty, / Since nature cannot choose his origin." Thus, external circumstances and intrinsic forces may constrain a man: he may be subject to inherited rank or to "particular fault" in a blood common to father, uncle, and nephew. Moreover, Shakespeare repeatedly places his view of beleaguered man in a larger context that reminds the reader of the flawed nature of man as a result of original sin: we are reminded that Adam was the first "grave-maker," the first "that ever bore arms" (V.i.35, 38); by such reminders, Shakespeare suggests that the act in the first garden reverberates in a world described as "an unweeded garden, / That grows to seed" (I.ii.135–36). But when we read of Claudius as a "serpent" that stings a father in a garden (I.v.39) and of Cain on whom "the primal eldest curse" (III.iii.37) was laid, we are reminded not only that man, like his father Adam, is subject to external attack and that as a result of his father's sin he contains a "vicious mole of nature" but also that in an ultimate sense he can be free, proof against all inner and outer restrictions.

And though Shakespeare points to conditions in existence that affect a man, to an imperfect nature and an imperfect world, a "goodly" prison (II.ii.251), his confinement imagery also presents the theme, common in Renaissance literature, that by a willing sin against rule and order, a man invites his own loss of liberty. The "imprisonment" of Pyrrhus, ruled by a desire to revenge the death of his father Achilles, is the result of his striking at a king and father. The spiritual entrapment that Claudius laments is the result of his own rejection of order—in subjecting reason to passion, in usurping the place of a king, in killing a brother. The reference to the heart brassed by damned custom appears in a scene where Hamlet not only discourses on the power of "that monster, custom," but also urges on Gertrude the assumption of a new "habit" and therefore indirectly indicates the role of the individual will in regard to custom and habit (III.iv.159–70). In the context of the situation in which each appears, such images as the imprisoned ear, the limed soul, and the brassed heart reflect the traditional view of the dangers inherent in improper choice and improper rule: all show the inevitable consequence of failing to adopt what Hamlet calls "the use of actions fair and good" (163).

So though the confinement images are all linked with evil, they appear to suggest a similar outcome for two dissimilar actions: that is, a kind of imprisonment may come to a man through no choice or sin of his own (the "loathsome crust") or through a willful choice of evil (the "limed soul"). But a subtle comment in the gravediggers' scene distinguishes between these two alternatives. And before determining to what degree each idea applies to all the figures assigning an imprisoned state to the Ghost or to Hamlet, let us stop to consider the choplogic of the First Clown when he says, "If the man go to this water, and drown himself, it is, will be, nill he, he goes, —mark you that; but if the water come to him and drown him, he drowns not himself: argal, he that is not guilty of his own death shortens not his own life" (V.i.17–22). Whatever the appearance of pompous nonsense in these words, one must remember that Shakespeare has had Hamlet insist on the large significance of clown scenes and criticize actors who obscure the playwright's art by setting "barren spectators to laugh . . . though, in the mean time, some necessary question of the play be then to be considered" (III.ii.46–48).

The Clown, of course, is pontificating on the circumstances of Ophelia's death and burial, and on a judgment of her guilt or innocence—whether her drowning can be called accident or suicide. But what he says is not applicable only to Ophelia: elsewhere in the play "going to the water" is connected with temptation and choice (see, for example, I.iv.69) and the oncoming of violence with images of flood (IV.v.99–102);[3] and elsewhere characters debate on suicide and the vicissitudes of chance and fate. Thus, underlying the Clown's words, how-

ever limited the context in which he uses them, is a consideration of questions of the play. Characteristically, Shakespeare
uses a Clown as a mouthpiece for serious comment: behind
the Clown's self-importance is an insistence on individual responsibility for wrong-doing and on the difference between
willingly (or even unwillingly) choosing evil and having evil
come to one, a difference that lies in eventual outcome and
ultimate judgment, however much it may appear that one
drowns either way. According to this "absolute" fellow, physical death is not the issue, but rather whether or not a man
makes the wrong choice: if he does, "will he, nill he," he must
bear an inevitable consequence; if he does not, he does not
"shorten . . . his own life," a life that denotes spiritual, as
well as physical, being. Thus, suicide takes on meanings that
extend beyond the literal definition. For all his pretentious
twaddle, the Clown is a medium for ideas that, as we shall
see, appear in various forms throughout the play; in speech
and action, he reveals that for him life is not something that
ends in the grave. And rot is not something that starts in the
grave: a man may, the Clown says, be "rotten before he die"
(V.i.181). So, in a large sense, an individual's health or sickness, his life or death, depends on his own choice—certainly
in this play "a necessary question . . . to be considered."

The Clown's words are relevant to the references to encrustment and confinement applied to Hamlet Senior. The
"prison-house" is the result of *his* action, of "foul crimes" that
must be purged from one "cut off even in the blossoms of
[his] sin" (I.v.12–13,76). But the *ultimate* effect of having
poison poured into his ears, of the evil that comes to him, is
not the scab he describes to Hamlet: the Ghost is not "bark'd
about, most lazar-like." It is rather the armor, which—unlike
the leprous crust—is an effect of his own choice. In the context of a potential for evil in custom (a constant concern of
the playwright), the danger of being "brass'd" by "damned
custom," certain emphases in the references to the armor are
most suggestive. That the Ghost is armed is a detail repeated
eight times. Of course, a martial appearance befits his mission; but that it is a natural elaboration of plot and tone for
a revengeful spirit to appear in arms hardly accounts for

Shakespeare's repeatedly pointing to the *extent* of the covering: the Ghost is encased "in complete steel" (I.iv.52); he is "armed at point exactly, cap-a-pe" (I.ii.200); he is "arm'd . . . From top to toe . . . from head to foot" (227–28). Moreover, the armor is, most significantly, given a history: Shakespeare identifies it as the "very armour" worn by King Hamlet in a duel thirty years before with King Fortinbras and thus links the present action with an earlier action that also elicited from the former King a response to ambition and "most emulate pride" (I.i.60–61,83); that resulted in the death of a king and father and—in the sense in which Hamlet later employs the word to Laertes (V.ii.255)—the death of a "brother." Perhaps we are intended to agree with Hamlet that *his* father's death is "particular" (I.ii.75) and to concur with him in all his later manifestations of this attitude—for example, when he, though seeing his father's violent death as abominable, sees the violent deaths of other men as, relatively, negligible matters. But I suspect that Shakespeare does not include such information in order to encourage us to make Hamlet our moral interpreter and that the identification of men who have been killed as kings, fathers, or brothers is not purposed to establish the "particularity" of one and the insignificance of another, whatever the variation in circumstances. In short, since confinement images are expressly the effect of Claudius's and Pyrrhus's killing of kings and fathers, in their case an undebatable evil, one is led to question the action of King Hamlet and to wonder whether the armour of the Ghost—given the odd reiterated emphasis on the extent of the covering—intimates a figurative, as well as a literal, encasement.[4]

Of course, there is great difference between King Fortinbras's challenge and Claudius's murder of a sleeping man and between the reactions that these deeds elicit in King Hamlet and the Ghost. (Yet, though there is also difference between King Hamlet's and King Priam's murders, their killers are, in various ways, associated.) What I am pointing to is the interlacing of ideas inherent in figure and fact: that, elsewhere, confinement follows on wrong choice; that the Ghost is not encrusted by a tetter, the effect of another man's evil, but by "complete steel," the effect of his own choice; that "the very armour" links this choice to an earlier one; that Shakespeare makes the present choice suspect by casting doubt on the earlier decision. Given all the differences between the two events, still Shakepeare stresses similarities: in describing the first, he insists on Norway's ambition, on King Hamlet's valiancy, and on the ratification of the duel by "law and heraldry" (I.i.61,83–87;ii.24–25). And however dissimilar the circumstances, the decision to bear arms against Claudius is also a reaction to ambition, a question of honor, and a response sanctioned by a knightly code. By directly connecting the two actions in the phrase "the very armour" and indirectly connecting them by way of other details that apply to both, Shakespeare can question the tenets of a particular custom and legality in the second action by questioning them in the first. And there is no doubt he gives us information that opens to debate both the practical wisdom in, and the moral justification for, trying to settle differences by violent means. For it is most significant that the first action did not end with the slaying of Norway. King Hamlet's earlier resort to this same "complete steel" produced the present danger of conflict: he "was and is the question of these wars" that threaten Denmark (I.i.111). Thus, the *chain-reacting* effect of the first response to aggression and its initial result—the death of a king, father, "brother"—suggest error, even though this method of handling an affair of honor had social and legal approval and no wrong was intended: "If the man go to this water, . . . it is, will he, nill he, he goes,—mark you that." The Ghost says that he is "confined" in consequence of "crimes," presumably sins against order and higher rule; and the emphasis on his "complete" encasement, joined to information that calls in question an earlier decision to don this same armor, supports the argument that a limitation of understanding and choice is still apparent in the unpurged and armed spirit whose customary response to aggression is violence and who does not invariably subscribe to the philosophy that vengeance should be left to Heaven.

If we apply the comment in the confinement imagery to Hamlet's finding Denmark a prison, the world a prison, and his thinking that he "lay / Worse than the mutines in the bilboes," we could say that the figurative language merely stresses the effect of Claudius's evil on those around him. On the other hand, if the "imprisoned ear" of Pyrrhus, the "limed soul" of Claudius, and the "prison-house" of the Ghost reflect the idea that being "cabin'd, cribb'd, confined" follows on one's own wrongdoing, the constraint of which Hamlet complains could express the same thought. And if the emphasis on the Ghost's encasement in steel implies a limitation attending wrong choice, a heart "brass'd" by "damned custom," then "prison" or "bilboes" could—if Hamlet submits to the rule of the Ghost—indicate the effect of that rule. But before considering whether either or both of these alternatives apply to Hamlet, let us confront more directly the question of the rightness or wrongness of the Ghost's mission, since Hamlet's failure to carry out the Ghost's charge immediately is so often considered a flaw and since such a view assumes either that the injunction is, in this play, proper ruling or that Hamlet, without any doubt, considers it so.

II

Just the fact that Hamlet Senior is a victim of "foul murder" would have been, in itself, enough to put us in his camp and to establish the starting point in an ordinary revenge play. But Shakespeare gives us details that deepen our pity for the Ghost and, at the same time, information that makes us dubious of his nature and mission.[5] The truth in his story, the circumstances of his death, his suffering, his plea to be remembered, his expressions of concern for Gertrude and Hamlet, his call on "nature," his appeal to filial love and loyalty, his majesty, his nobility—all enlist our sympathy. But an important theme in the play, a theme expounded just before the Ghost's appearance to Hamlet, is that the noble substance may be corrupted by habit, by fortune, by intrinsic flaw. And the Ghost may have justice on his side, exhibit noble qualities, arouse our sympathies, and still be wrong.

We have noted certain details that Shakespeare inserts about King Hamlet (his martial exploits; his killing a king and father; his "sin" and "crimes") and about the Ghost (his foulness not yet purged by the flames of his prison-house; his insistence that Horatio and Marcellus swear by the sword, rather than by their faith). We have noted Shakespeare's placement of the scene in which the Ghost enjoins Hamlet to revenge (just after Polonius's questionable charges to Laertes and Ophelia and just before his cynical instruction to Reynaldo) and his placement of the Ghost's materializations (to Horatio on the heels of a speech about disaster and sickness; to Hamlet on words about a dram of evil; in Gertrude's closet, at the phrase "a king of shreds and patches"). We have seen that the ear/speech imagery, the noise symbolism, and the confinement figures suggest that his tale and call for revenge may be a poison and their effect a confinement; and we have noted a considerable number of figurative recurrences that associate him with corruption, disease, decay: his being called "old mole" after a speech about a corrupting "mole of nature"; his being linked with "blastments" and therefore with contagion; his being described as "blast[ed]" by a "mildew'd ear" and therefore himself a transmitter of mildew. Moreover, when he compares himself with Claudius (I.v.47–52), he displays vanity, and his analogy indirectly identifying himself with "a radiant angel" plays fast and loose with the facts of "prison-house" and "flames." It might also be tentatively noted that if the stage direction in the Second Quarto on the time of cockcrow is placed as Shakespeare intended, the exhortation of Horatio that moves the Ghost to speak (he "was about to speak, when the cock crew") is "If thou hast uphoarded in thy life / Exhorted treasure in the womb of earth, / For which, they say, you spirits oft walk in death, / Speak" (I.i.147,136–39): a reply to this particular *if* is in line with the information that the former King took land from King Fortinbras and that the Ghost is "doom'd . . . to walk the night" (I.v.10).

The cumulative force of all this makes it difficult to see the Ghost as a typical spirit of the revenge drama whose mission is to be accepted without question. And there is a telling identification of the Ghost's nature in other references to cockcrow. When Shakespeare stresses the effect of the latter on the Ghost by having the same information given by three characters (I.i.147–49,157;ii.218–20); when he has Horatio say that "at the sound" the Ghost "started like a guilty thing" and that he has heard that "at [the cock's] warning . . . The extravagant and erring spirit hies / To his confine" (I.i.148, 152–55); when he has Marcellus add emphatically that the Ghost "faded on the crowing of the cock" (157), and later has the Ghost say that he is "confined" during the day (I.v. 11)—then only the most willful defenders of the Ghost can discount the logical conclusion that he is, however noble, also an "extravagant and erring spirit." Both fact and figure tell us that he is flawed, blasted, in need of purging. The corruption that he took in life from "nature's livery" and "fortune's star," the customs that he espoused, his "habit as he lived,"[6] the crimes and sins that brought him to the flames of the prison-house—all are still operating in the unpurged spirit. Even to those he would not have "tainted" he is a threat: for like a man with plague who does not intentionally transmit the disease, he endangers the health of all he comes near.

Finally, an assumption that the Ghost exhibits order, rather than extravagance and error, and that his ruling is proper does not take into account the fact that the aristocratic code of honor and justice is not the only, or the noblest, standard of conduct set forth in the play. When Hamlet tells Polonius to "let [the players] be well used" and Polonius answers, "I will use them according to their desert," Hamlet says, "God's bodykins, man, much better: use every man after his desert, and who should 'scape whipping? Use them after your own honour and dignity: the less they deserve, the more merit is in your bounty. Take them in" (II.ii.547–58).[7] However sympathetically Shakespeare may present certain primitive ideals of justice and duty, however much he may have his protagonist berate himself for not acting in accord with them, we cannot assume in this play—as we might in a drama where summary violent retribution for evil is the only acceptable action and where the hero conceives of nothing nobler— that a failure to take prompt revenge is a flaw. The Ghost enjoins Hamlet to treat Claudius according to his desert; but if Shakespeare shows us a Hamlet who believes (whatever else he believes) that treating a man so is not tantamount to treating him according to honor and dignity, then the matter of proper action is complicated. At the very least, we are not justified in concluding that Shakespeare presents, and that Hamlet esteems, only one standard of conduct.

A. C. Bradley says that Hamlet "habitually assumes . . . that he *ought* to avenge his father" and that "we are meant . . . to assume" the same.[8] This makes the question "Why does Hamlet hesitate?" the whole dramatic problem, not just one aspect of a larger problem; and it must inevitably produce only subjective opinions about the nature of the protagonist. Too many critics have revealed an unwillingness to take into account *all* of Hamlet's words and actions (or his words in relation to his deeds, or his words about other characters in relation to their deeds); thus (since in the end they must deal with Shakespeare's play and not their own attenuated version) simplifying the course of *Hamlet*, they have created their own blind alleys. In saying that we are meant to assume that Hamlet ought to avenge his father, Bradley has to disregard the *fact* that Hamlet voices to Polonius a philosophy of conduct that runs directly counter to that of revenge. And surely Shakespeare does not purposelessly point to a rule morally superior to that which Bradley says we are to assume is the proper standard.

The fact is that we are given a protagonist who expresses views that are polar opposites (one should/should not treat a man according to his deserts) and whose actions are as contradictory as his words. Obviously, we cannot say that Hamlet's failure to carry out the Ghost's charge immediately proves that he does not esteem a code of revenge; nor can we say that his justification of the killing of Rosencrantz and Guildenstern on the score of their receiving their just due proves that he does not esteem the rule of charity he expresses to Polonius. We *can* say that in the light of one code to which he subscribes he "assumes that he ought to avenge his father." Yet he questions more than just the truth in the Ghost's story; as late as the fifth act, when he no longer has any doubt of Claudius's guilt, he is still mingling observations about killing the King with allusions to conscience and damnation and putting them in question form (V.ii.67–70). He may put conscience on the scale with the Ghost and damnation on the side of inaction, and he may iterate the question to propel himself to action; but a harping on defenses for killing is not characteristic of one who "assumes" that no defense is needed. We *can* say that he does not explicitly apply to the Ghost's injunction the philosophy that he himself enjoins on Polonius; but this should not lead the critic to conclude that his words to Polonius are irrelevant to the whole matter. Actually, the fact that he makes no connection between principle and practice is, like his speaking disparagingly of dumb shows and then sponsoring one, most significant: Shakespeare does not repeatedly show Hamlet's words at odds with his action to no purpose. Hamlet voices a noble philosophy to Polonius. And the standard of action that he urges on the worldly old man is but one instance of a recurrent comment on an ideal rule far more difficult to put into practice than that which the Ghost urges on him.

In coming to conclusions about what Hamlet does or does not "assume," we cannot discount his expressed double-mindedness on the matter of treatment and desert: it may have some bearing on his difficulty in dispatching a single-minded action. And as to what *we* should or should not suppose, when Shakespeare presents a philosophy that admonishes, even indirectly, against revenge, when he shows us that even Claudius's appeal to Norway succeeds in thwarting war between Denmark and a vengeful Fortinbras, then we are not "meant to assume" that revenge is the better choice or violence the only option. The very presence in the play of an expression of a philosophy morally superior to that of revenge, along with all of the other details that cast doubt on the nature and mission of the Ghost, reinforces the argument that the rule of the Ghost is wrong and that if Hamlet accepts it, "will he, nill he," he makes the wrong choice.

Shakespeare repeatedly evokes questions of rule. We see Hamlet, Laertes, and Fortinbras, who all suffer the deaths of fathers, reacting differently to *explicit* overtures of rule. Hamlet replies to the plea, "Be ruled" (when Horatio warns him against listening to the Ghost), with "I'll make a ghost of him that lets me!" (I.v.81,85), and thus with a violent threat to create more ghosts, refuses to be ruled. Laertes replies to

Claudius's "Will you be ruled by me?" (when revenge for a father's death is the question) with "Ay, my lord; / So you will not o'errule me to a peace" (IV.vii.60–61). But Fortinbras, who has "shark'd up a list of lawless resolutes," accepts the ruling of his uncle Norway and vows not to "give the assay of arms" against Denmark (I.i.98;II.ii.71). And in this tragedy framed by two duels, it is the man who accepts a ruling for peace and who allows himself to be "o'erruled" to that end, who becomes ruler—at least, the one on whom election will presumably light (V.ii.366–67), though this outcome has its own built-in ironies.

But does Hamlet, who refuses to be guided by Marcellus and Horatio, accept the rule of the Ghost? Since Horatio fears that the Ghost may "tempt [Hamlet] toward the flood," the question may be restated in the words of the First Clown: does he go to the water? A case may be made for the alternative, that the water comes to him to drown him: quite aside from the recurrent allusions to the constraint in "nature's livery [and] fortune's star," in birth and blood, in "the whips . . . of time [and] The oppressor's wrong," Shakespeare significantly places three events in one day—the birth of Hamlet, the slaying of King Fortinbras, and the First Clown's coming to the profession of grave-digger (V.i.154–62). Such a juxtaposition suggests the importance of fate in Hamlet's tragedy. And in a most crucial particular, Hamlet is obviously not ruled by the Ghost: the killing of Claudius is finally occasioned by the death of the Queen, Hamlet's discovery that *he* has been poisoned, the evidence before him of the truth in Laertes', not the Ghost's, accusation—in short, by the present and manifest treachery of Claudius.

But if one can say that he only casually accomplishes the bidding of the Ghost, one cannot say that he observes the admirable rules of conduct that he himself lays down for others. And in determining whether, by the confinement figures describing his state, Shakespeare suggests the effect of wrong choice and improper rule, one must consider the discrepancy between Hamlet's own preaching and his practice. "Suit the action to the word," he tells the First Player (III. ii.19–20); and the advice has ironic extensions as he is repeatedly seen in actions not suited to his own words. His putting on an "antic disposition" gives his counsel to the players and his criticism of them angles of reflection and reverberation that Shakespeare brilliantly exploits to stress the difference between what Hamlet says and what he does, between his wisdom and his perception of a practical application of that wisdom.[9] He says of the child players, "Will they not say afterward, if they should grow themselves to common players . . . their writers do them wrong, to make them exclaim against their own succession?" (II.ii.363–68). Yet after his Ghost writer writes his part, he is preoccupied with exclaiming against his own succession, whether as prince or human being.

Over and over, Hamlet gives good counsel and "recks not his own rede" (I.iii.51). Considering his usual treatment of Polonius, it is peculiarly ironic that he should address Polonius as "man" (the only time he does so in the play) when urging on him noble behavior to all men, though considering the devious old counselor's own penchant for lecturing and adopting moral stances, it is fitting that he should be so instructed by one who usually treats him with contempt; and it is doubly ironic, in view of Polonius's dubious conception of honor, that he should be told to treat every man according to his "own honour and dignity." However, Hamlet intends no irony; for once, he addresses Polonius without scorn or ridicule (and it is significant that his unwonted decency of tone to the old man follows on Polonius's expression of concern for the First Player: "Look, whether he has not turned his colour and has tears in 's eyes. Pray you, no more"). But sincere as Hamlet's counsel may be, one does not see him "take [men] in," at least not in the sense of the "bounty" he advocates to Polonius. In another striking manifestation of inconsistency, he tells the Players not to mock Polonius (II.ii.570–71). That he, the only person in the court who habitually subjects Polonius to derision, should give such a direction attests to his self-contradiction; but Shakespeare underscores the point by placing this command to the Players shortly after a passage where *mockery* precisely describes Hamlet's own treatment of Polonius: the latter says, "My lord, I have news to tell you," and Hamlet mimics him, "My lord, I have news to tell you," and so on, with a jeering "Buz, buz!" when Polonius tells him that the actors have arrived (407–12). Moreover, he says wise words to Horatio about the potential corruption in "habit" and repeats them to Gertrude; yet he puts on the habit of madness and does not apply to himself his recommendation to Gertrude of "the use of actions fair and good." Again, he expounds on the danger in "that monster, custom, who all sense doth eat" (III.iv.161); but he commends the custom of revenge for an injury done a kinsman and justifies his plot against the lives of his former schoolfellows on an approximation of the old custom of an eye for an eye.

Besides contradicting his own preachments, he repeatedly goes counter to his expressed convictions, sentiments, and predilections; and again and again he criticizes others for faults that he exhibits. Often he gives lip service to a conduct that he, at that very moment (or shortly after or before) denies in action. Expressing scorn for dumb shows and then sponsoring a play that contains one, declaring trust in Horatio and then refusing to accept a vow that Horatio swears by his faith—such behavior is typical of Hamlet. He often denounces seeming: early in the play he says, "I know not 'seems' " (I.ii. 76); yet he puts on seeming with the antic disposition and not only practices deception as busily as anyone else in the court but even displays some pride in his talent at it (see, for example, III.ii.286–89;V.ii.35–36). Similarly, he criticizes Ophelia and women for their misrepresentation of truth: "God has given you one face, and you make yourselves another" (III.i.149–50); yet he has made himself another face and put on the mask of madness. He censures Ophelia and women for "nicknam[ing] God's creatures" (151); but he himself is peculiarly given to this fault,[10] and it is not shown to be characteristic of either Ophelia or Gertrude. On several occasions, he declares a dislike for rant (see III.ii.8–16;V.i.306–7, ii.79–80); yet in the passage where, in his opinion, Laertes rants, he himself indulges in twice as many lines of rant as Laertes. While it is atypical that he should, in this same passage, express an awareness of doing what he censures, it is characteristic that he extenuates *his* ranting as appropriate response to Laertes, as if it were not a chronic reaction of his own. Again, he finds the fact that his father was sent to his death "unhousel'd" a matter of especial horror and wickedness, an opinion he shares with the Ghost (cf.I.v.76–80 and III. iii.80–82); yet he wants Claudius's punishment to exceed measure-for-measure (III.iii.88–95), and he specifies that Rosencrantz and Guildenstern be slain without "shriving-time allow'd" (V.ii.47).

We shall have occasion to point to other instances of the contradiction between Hamlet's words and actions or between his words at one time and at another. Since too many critics see only the failure that Hamlet talks about—"Why yet [he] live[s] to say 'This thing's to do;' / Sith [he has] cause and will and strength and means / To do't" (IV.iv.44–46)—his failure to act on a rule that he prescribes for other men or that he intimates as proper by way of his criticism of those around him cannot be too strongly insisted on. Some critics have actually wondered at Shakespeare's inconsistency in having Hamlet conjecture on "the dread of something after death" (III.i.78) when he has talked with the Ghost. But it is not Shakespeare who is inconsistent. Hamlet is invariably portrayed as a man who sees all things that relate to him as "particular"; and his increasingly strange distinction between reality for himself and reality for others manifests itself in a variety of ways. If it accommodates his purpose to see himself as sharing in a common human nature, he will evoke that condition, but for an extenuation of his own fault or, paradoxically, to establish his difference from other men. When he criticizes himself, it is, characteristically, in the largest terms: "I am very proud, revengeful, ambitious, with more offences at my beck than I have thoughts to put them in," he tells Ophelia; but he adds, "We are arrant knaves, all" (126–30,132). Even in sin he is exceptional; yet, after all, his sins reflect the human condition: his sins are the sins of mankind. But when he criticizes the shortcomings of those around him, their sins are not his: there is no indication that he sees in himself the fault, for example, of nicknaming God's creatures, ranting, or making himself another face—at least, not without the qualification that such actions are "particular" with him, not to be identified with the common failings of other men. One never gets the idea that Hamlet does not sincerely believe in the admirable conduct that he, in words if not in deeds, presents to others. It is quite clear that he recoils from evil; but it is also clear that he does not apply to his own action a knowledge and a conception of higher rule that he is capable of applying to the character and action of other people. In time, this failure becomes a fatal one. It is one thing to fail, either wittingly or unwittingly, to live up to one's own definition of proper rule. But it is quite another to insist explicitly on two definitions of proper rule, one for other men and another for one's self, the latter to be determined by what one wills to do. To say that Hamlet moves to this interpretation of reality may be an oversimplification of the facts, but it is not an overstatement of them. In time, his own action, even when it is similar to that which he rejects in other men, becomes in his mind a basis for defining the rule of Heaven, rather than the other way around.

In part, Hamlet's sense of reality is corrupted by the practice of *show;* and one of Shakespeare's basic tenets in *Hamlet* is the self-destructive nature of false-seeming. It has been said that Hamlet does not act, simply because he does not immediately kill Claudius—in short, because *he* says he does not act. And it might be inferred from this that he does not accept the rule of the Ghost. But he chooses the role of actor and, putting on the mask and and action of madness, "acts" until he no longer draws a line between reality and unreality. He may not "sweep to [the] revenge" the Ghost wants, but he becomes the busiest gravemaker in Elsinore, a consequence implying that his "noble substance" *has* been poisoned by what he interprets as an injunction to kill. And the mask itself, which follows immediately on the Ghost's charge, demonstrates the contaminating effect of an unreality that Shakespeare finds in words and acts that enjoin to violence. Hamlet eventually disclaims to Laertes "a purposed evil" (V.ii.252); but in the scene where a "necessary question of the play [is] . . . considered," Shakespeare has the First Clown insist on the irrevocable nature of the *act,* whether intentional or not: "If the man go to this water, . . . will he, nill he, he goes." Moreover, however unpurposed the wrong done Laertes, Hamlet willfully contrives deaths "not near [his] conscience" (58), although he also contrives in connection with them circumstances that he himself has declared particularly evil.

In the deterioration of Hamlet's sense of proportion and reality, one sees the spreading of evil from the little dram, the vial of poison. He is, in part, a victim, encrusted by a poisonous element that enters his ears: so he finds Denmark a prison and the world a prison just after he is told of his father's murder and given the accompanying charge. But whether he considers its relevance to his own problem or not, he is also aware of a course of action contrary to that advocated by the Ghost. The almost insurmountable difficulties of putting an ideal of charity into practice, given the circumstances, or the form it could take in a practical world of ugly realities—these are not, at present, our concern. Considering merely the logic of the confinement imagery, we are faced with certain uncompromising facts: Hamlet voices a philosophy that runs directly counter to the philosophy of treating a man according to his deserts; it is a rule morally superior to that espoused by the Ghost; and Hamlet does not choose to be ruled by it. Thus, his feeling of confinement to "bilboes" immediately before he plots the death of his former friends is in line with the figurative comment elsewhere in the play on the imprisoning effect of wrong rule and suggests the circumscription of understanding and choice manifested *as he puts into action the Ghost's philosophy of revenge.* A strict study of the confinement imagery leads to two conclusions: one, he is confined by a "vile and loathsome crust" that comes from evil circumstance and evil times; the other, the confinement that matters, is a consequence of his own act, as he willfully rejects the rule he exhorts Polonius to follow: "Use [men] after your own honour and dignity: the less they deserve, the more merit is in your bounty. Take them in."

By now some of my readers, in defense of Hamlet, may be damning this argument out of hand before they hear the end of it; and others who second D. H. Lawrence's "And Hamlet, how boring, how boring to live with, / So mean and self-conscious, blowing and snoring / His wonderful speeches, full of other folk's whoring!"[11] may be giving it an approval they will eventually revoke. But whatever opinions one may finally have of Hamlet's character and whatever conclusions one may reach about what happens in *Hamlet*, one must come to them without ignoring or whitewashing his faults and without slighting his nobility. Robert Ornstein says, "Our moral impression of Hamlet's character derives primarily from what he says rather than what he does," an observation that sums up one common critical reaction and explains the rationale of many critics who identify with Hamlet despite his "brutality towards Ophelia, his reaction to Polonius' death, . . . his Machiavellian delight in disposing of Rosencrantz and Guildenstern."[12] But, as Lawrence's lines prove, even what Hamlet says does not give all readers the same moral impression. And although Professor Ornstein is much more objective than many commentators who take Hamlet for their moral interpretater, he discounts the impression that Hamlet's actions obviously make on him when he argues that Shakespeare leads us to judge Hamlet primarily by his words. But Shakespeare does not take great pains to establish a contradiction between Hamlet's words and actions to lead us to attend to only one method of revealing character; *he* does not characterize Hamlet only by his words, or only by his actions, or only by some of his words, some of his actions. If brainwashed by Hamlet's eloquence, his greatness of mind, his suffering, we view him like "barren spectators," using only his eyes, we may do him an injustice and, paradoxically, not see to the depths of his recoil from Claudius's evil, the killing of a king and kinsman. But if we equivocate, ignore his violation of his own high standards of conduct and the confinement figures relevant to a breach of proper rule, pick and choose among his words and deeds, and excuse his violence and savagery because he has had great provocation and speaks so well, we do *Hamlet* an injustice.

Taking the stand that one must find a moral justification for anything that Hamlet or the Ghost *does* may lead to the kind of argument set forth by one critic who says that since God permits the Ghost to revisit the earth, "the Ghost's demand . . . is . . . the transmission of a divine command."[13] The idea that what God allows, he commands, puts Claudius's murder of King Hamlet in a startling perspective and offers a sweeping resolution of the whole problem of good and evil. But if it were true, one would have to believe that because such criticism is permitted, it is therefore divinely ordained. And one must draw a line somewhere.

CHAPTER FIVE

I

A beast/trap imagery extends the figurative comment on confinement. The repeated resort of the principal characters to the setting of traps; the reiterated metaphorical allusion to trap, springe, toil, basket, and angle; the recurrent beast-figures describing, not only the quarry, but also those who hunt and fish for others of their breed—all provide further comment on the nature, operation, and effect of evil and point to a wholesale moral failure in the society of Elsinore. An objective consideration of the beast and the trap imagery enables the reader to avoid partial conclusions about the drama: for example, at one end of the critical spectrum, the view that Claudius is the complete villain of the piece, the source of all evil in Denmark, and Hamlet representative of divine forces; at the other end, the view that Claudius is "a good and gentle king, enmeshed by the chain of causality" and Hamlet a "poison" in the "healthy bustle" of the court.[1]

Except for Fortinbras and others who appear briefly in the action, every character in the play is, at one time or another, described in a beast-image. The most frequently employed figure is that of a winged thing, usually a bird; and it is applied almost always to the young people in the play. Significantly, the exception is Claudius: when he describes his soul

77

as limed, one is reminded of a trap for birds; and he is called a bat, a pajock, perhaps indirectly a hawk. However, aside from these (and *bat* is, as we shall see, allied to another image cluster) and perhaps the figure of the "buzzers" who "infect [Laertes'] ear," the winged-creature image is not evoked for the old, though it is directly or indirectly applied to every member of the younger generation. Whether the likenesses are suggested by metaphor or simile, whether they are explicit or implicit labels, the following similarities are drawn: Ophelia and Laertes are called woodcocks (I.iii.115;V.ii.317); Laertes a pelican (IV.v.146); Horatio a bird (I.v.115); Hamlet, who questions whether he is pigeon-livered, a female dove (II.ii.605;V.i.309);[2] Osric a waterfly, a chough, and a lapwing (V.ii.84,89,194). Even the child players described by Rosencrantz are called an aerie of little eyases (II.ii.355). When Hamlet, at the end of his first talk with Rosencrantz and Guildenstern, says, "I know a hawk from a handsaw" (397), it might be argued that he indirectly applies a hawk-image to his former schoolfellows.[3] But if the line does comment on their nature, it is more likely that he identifies them with "handsaws" (*and* hernshaws): seeing his old friends as Claudius's tools, he declares that he (unlike Rosencrantz, who calls the tools of the writers little hawks) does not confuse a predator like Claudius with a Rosencrantz or a Guildenstern.[4]

However that may be, the winged-creature figures do put the young people in the play in a category with Claudius. And though the traits thus ascribed to them (for example, the stupidity of the woodcock, the timidity of the pigeon, the triviality of the waterfly, the chattering of the chough, the silly activity of the lapwing, even the latent predaciousness of the little eyases) may not suggest the full-blown evil in the bat or pajock figures describing Claudius, still this figurative category is employed, for the most part, to diminish the human character rather than to aggrandize it.[5] Furthermore, the same figure is used elsewhere only in descriptions of passion, undesirable circumstance, or questionable action: of hot love (II.ii.132), melancholy and danger (III.i.173–75), and secrecy (II.ii.305–6); in a description of the immature and untried: "new-hatch'd, unfledged comrade" (I.iii.65); and in a slant description of players, rather disparagingly characterized in the phrase "a forest of feathers" (III.ii.286). Even those figures that, in the immediate context, are inoffensively or favorably intended (see, for example, I.v.115;IV.v.146;V.i. 309) do not dispel the force of the whole pattern suggesting that a character identified as a creature inferior to man errs against order and, capable of flight, debases a nature potentially "in action . . . like an angel."

Another group of beast-images is used only in description of the older generation: Gertrude is called a mouse (III.iv. 183); Polonius a rat (23) in an epithet intended for Claudius; and Claudius a bat, a mouse-like creature (190). According to a beast lore still familiar in Shakespeare's day, the mole is sometimes described as a mouse;[6] whether or not such lore invests the "old mole" with traits evoked in descriptions of Gertrude, Polonius, and Claudius, we shall find that there *are* connections between the Ghost and the mouse-figure. And in a play where a dramatic performance is a trap, intended— so the trapper says—to "catch the conscience of the king," and where that drama is called "The Mouse-trap," the mouse-image is important, a point we shall consider when we turn from a categorizing of beast-figures to the question of their significance.

The purpose of the character who applies an image to another character may not add up to the purpose of the playwright who gives him the words. Still, it is instructive simply to note what characters are linked by the same figurative label. The word *beast* is used in descriptions of Claudius and Pyrrhus (I.v.42;II.ii.472), whose descents from a proper human nature are defined in similar actions. But *beast* also becomes an alternative name for Osric (ostensibly a far cry from "hellish" killers) and for a general citizenry: "Let a beast be lord of beasts, and his crib shall stand at the king's mess" (V.ii.87– 89). The serpent-image is used only to identify Claudius and Rosencrantz and Guildenstern (I.v.39;III.iv.203); the ape-image only for Claudius and Gertrude (III.iv.194;IV.ii.19). It will be recalled that Hamlet links forgotten men (and he has been speaking of his father) with the hobbyhorse character in the Morris Dance. Shortly thereafter, in "Let the galled jade wince, our withers are unwrung" (III.ii.252–53), he summons up the horse-figure, most pointedly for Claudius, but also for himself; still later, he again suggests this image for himself in the phrase "While the grass grows," the unspoken conclusion of the proverb being, "the silly horse starves" (358–59). So all three representatives of the Danish royal house are, in some sense, linked with the horse-figure. There are other suggestive equivalences. The Danish rabble who cry, "Laertes shall be king" are labeled false dogs (IV.v.110); soon after this, Laertes, who leads this "riotous head," is implicitly called dog (and cat) when Hamlet, after asking why Laertes should rant against him, says contemptuously, "Let Hercules himself do what he may, / The cat will mew and dog will have his day" (V.i.314–15;).[7] Circumstance and the pattern of the references to Hercules suggest that *dog* and *cat* may also here be slant descriptions of Claudius, king of the "false Danish dogs," a king whose guilt must be "unkennel[ed]" (III.ii.86) and who is also elsewhere called gib (III.iv.190). A calf-image is used for Polonius (III.ii.111); and men who seek safety in parchments are called calves and sheep (V.i.125). An ass-image is employed by Hamlet to describe himself (II.ii.611), by Hamlet for the First Clown (V.i.87), and indirectly by the First Clown for the Second Clown (64). Other beast-images characterize only one person: Hamlet calls Claudius a paddock (III.iv.190); he likens himself to a lion (I.iv.83) and a fox (IV.ii.32) and, indirectly, to a chameleon (III.ii.98). A number of the images of winged things noted above (pelican, water-fly, chough, lapwing, pajock, bird) appear only once.[8]

For the most part, the limited meaning of this imagery—that is, the intent of the speaker—is obvious: sometimes an adjective points to the trait the figure echoes—the lion is "hardy," the dog "false," the dove "patient." Generally, intrinsic qualities of the animal inform the image: for example, the venomous nature of the adder; the predacity of the hawk; the wiliness of the fox; the stupidity of calf or ass. If one considers only a few of the labels that Hamlet applies to Claudius, context and connotation leave no doubt as to his meaning: the King is invested with the falsehood of serpent and dog; the vanity and lust of pajock and gib; the loathsomeness of the paddock. Although the immediate significance of most of the epithets requires no belaboring, their meaning is often enriched if one takes into account a ready-made symbolism in the beast lore. Shakespeare shows his familiarity with this literature when Hamlet says that he "eat[s] the air" like the chameleon and when Laertes likens himself to the "life-rendering pelican." The lore that apes are given to "deceits, impostures and flatteries" and that mice are "infidious . . . deceitful" and "in general most libidinous," the female "more venereous than the male," appropriately informs all uses of these particular images. Similarly, "old mole" is a suggestive name for the Ghost in the light of a traditional teaching: to wit, moles are "all blinde . . . and therefore came the proverb . . . to signifie a man without all judgement, wit or foresight"; it should "never enter into the heart of a reasonable man, that such beasts can love Religion." Certainly, the belief that cats "in the time of Pestilence are not only apt to bring home venemous infection, but to poison a man with very looking upon him"[9] lends a peculiar suitability to such a name for Laertes and Claudius.

Such lore may accommodate the speaker's meaning, as when Hamlet links Claudius with the ape; or it may charge the epithet with meanings not intended by the speaker, as when Hamlet employs the term "old mole" for the Ghost. The three names he assigns to himself—lion, when he declares his hardiness; ass, when he laments his neglect of the dictates of an aristocratic concept of honor; fox, when he plays the elusive trickster—recall "that pretty fable of *Esope*" telling how these three beasts entered into "league." But when the Lion commanded the Ass to make division of a certain booty, "the silly Asse regarding nothing but societie . . . and not honor and dignity, parted the same into three equall shares," whereat the Lion "toar him to pieces" and then gave the job to the Fox. That wily beast satisfied the Lion's view of honor and dignity by assigning him almost all of the booty.[10] "Honour and dignity" are the qualities Hamlet specifies as the basis for determining one's treatment of one's fellows (II.ii.556–57), though (as we have noted) the "bounty" that he urges on Polonius is hardly in line with the conduct that reflects honor and dignity in the eyes of the Ghost. If this familiar lore does inform the choice of beast-figures for Hamlet, Shakespeare is manipulating the ironies inherent in the fable: though Hamlet, unlike both Lion and Ass, does implicitly link "honour and dignity" with society in his little lecture, he is also as capable as the beasts in the fable of finding them incompatible; and the eventual machinations of the fox Hamlet echo the progress of the old tale.

The beast imagery provides comment on the describer, as well as the person described. Since of the forty-odd instances listed above where a man is called a beast, three-fourths of them appear in Hamlet's speech, they spotlight the character of the man who censures other men for "nick-nam[ing] God's creatures." Second, since he does not restrict his name-calling to Claudius but manages to fasten a beast-image on every principal character in the play and, on at least one occasion, to designate a whole group of human beings as beasts, we are repeatedly given his opinion of his own kind,[11] and also perhaps a qualification, to some degree, of his opinion of Claudius, since he includes so many others in the same category. Third, and most important, Hamlet's use of these figures reveals a progressive change in his character. Not once before his encounter with the Ghost does he describe a fellow man as a beast. Polonius and the Ghost do; but in the first act Hamlet expresses a distaste for such epithets. As we have seen, he tells Horatio that men of other nations "with swinish phrase / Soil [the Danes'] addition"; disapproving the custom that produces the label, he apparently disapproves of the labeling as well. At least, "swinish phrase" accommodates a twofold meaning—that the Danes are called swine and that such name-calling is swinish. His own first employment of a "swinish phrase" follows on his first meeting with the Ghost. Between that time and the death of Polonius, though the habit of applying abusive names to other men grows on him, he does not often directly and explicitly "soil [their] addition" by calling them beasts; and he applies such language to himself as often as to others. But with the presentation of the court entertainment, his use of such a comparison begins to increase; and after the killing of Polonius, the practice becomes habitual. Of the twenty-four epithets listed above that occur between the time Hamlet stabs at the arras and the end of the play, seventeen are employed by him; only one of these refers to himself, and all of the others are abusive.

Perhaps in another way the beast images provide comment on the describer. The only characters who identify others in exactly the same words are Laertes and Polonius (woodcock), Hamlet and the Ghost (beast), Hamlet and Gertrude (dog), and Hamlet and the First Clown (ass). Certain similarities between Laertes and his father and between Hamlet and his parents can hardly be denied. Whether Shakespeare intends to reinforce such likenesses by assigning to parent and son the same language is a moot question; nevertheless, the repetition, if fortuitous, effects a comparison. Similarly, when Hamlet laments that he is an ass, then (in lines taking for granted his unlikeness to the one described) applies the same name to a Clown who has just applied it to another Clown, the re-iteration—if chance—is still happily and ironically illustrative of a repeated thematic comment that a man may see the mote in the other fellow's eye, but not in his own—at least, not see that it is the same mote.

The imagery often affords Shakespeare ironic comment on the action. That Polonius warns Laertes against the "new-hatch'd, unfledged comrade"; that Laertes later declares himself ready to imitate the bird who repasts her new-hatched brood with her blood; and that eventually Laertes has, as go-between for a duel to result in his death, a lapwing who "runs away with the shell on his head" (V.ii.193–94)—all this, if again chance, is the luckiest of figurative interplay. Similarly, Polonius's describing himself as a player who was "killed i' the Capitol" in the role of Julius Caesar and Hamlet's immediately calling him a calf foreshadows the event where Polonius's foolish plotting leads to the calf's being sacrificed again, this time in the capitol of Denmark in a different kind of play role when he is mistakenly assigned the part of tyrant by the killer. Again, Hamlet's describing himself as "hardy as the Nemean lion" in the face of any potential danger in an encounter with the Ghost has ironic overtones in its echo of one of his own earlier speeches: he has declared that Claudius is no more like King Hamlet than he [Hamlet] is like Hercules (I.ii.152–53). Such an analogy implies not only difference between the two brothers and between Hamlet and Hercules but also a similarity between King Hamlet and Hercules; thus, when Hamlet draws a likeness between himself and the lion killed by Hercules (I.iv.82–83), he unwittingly stresses the danger to him in the situation, rather than his strength to withstand harm.[12]

In the scene where Osric delivers Laertes' challenge and is himself baited, Hamlet's characterization of the messenger twice hinges on a characterization of the age (see V.ii.87–89; 196–97); and Osric's conduct serves, in turn, to define the nature of those with whom he is figuratively identified. He is, Hamlet says, "of the same breed that . . . the drossy age dotes on" (V.ii.196–97). If we are to judge by Hamlet's descriptions of him, it is a beastly breed. If we are to judge by Osric's own words and actions, it is a breed marked by an extravagant and insubstantial speech, a taste for show, an indiscriminate regard for form and custom, a pretense to excellence, a lack of understanding. Aspects of his verbal exchange with Hamlet provide peculiar (if limited) warrant for Hamlet's extending his judgment of Osric to a judgment of the court; for whether consciously or not, Hamlet establishes points of similarity between the foolish young courtier and a foolish old one to whom he also has repeatedly affixed beast labels and whose "crib" also stood "at the king's mess." In his wordiness, Osric is not unlike Polonius; and Hamlet, employing *exactly* the technique he used in baiting the prolix chamberlain, leads Osric into *exactly* the same compliant self-contradiction (cf. III.ii.393–99;V.ii.97–104). Also, as Hamlet mimicked Polonius (see II.ii.408–9), he apes Osric, if not in the same fashion; and Osric's ears are assailed by a parody of his own extravagance, as earlier the equivocator Polonius was treated to equivocation or as the old "buzzer" and infector of ears had the sound of gossip returned to him in Hamlet's "Buz, buz!" Such mimicry vividly (albeit ambiguously) illustrates the recoil of speech or action on its source, a significant motif in this play. And by echoing Osric's nonsense to his confusion, Hamlet contemptuously makes him bear witness to the lack of understanding and rule behind his facade of words.[13]

In important part because of the figurative equations that Hamlet belabors, his exposé of Osric's lack of substance provides a perspective on his own nature; and the inanity, compliance, and ignorance that he holds up to scorn invite comparisons that he cannot intend. One remembers that "some necessary question of the play" may be considered by way of a Clown when one sees that certain scales do not tip when the lightweight Osric is balanced against men of more force. Osric's penchant for "golden words" (V.ii.136) may take a different form from the moral maxims of Polonius, the sensible argument that Claudius is capable of voicing, the high wisdom of Hamlet; still, his silly talk is no less empty than admirable speech denied in action. Osric may be trifling, but he is of the "same breed" as Polonius, similarly given to art without matter (II.ii.95); as Claudius, with whom he is identified by the word *beast;* even as the bird Hamlet, who recognizes no point of relationship between himself and this "chough" whose chatter falls so far short of his own wit. Posturing, false-seeming, the utterance of sound without substance are characteristics insistently connected with the beast, and the beastliness of the court is reflected in the counterfeit speech and action of this frivolous courtier who, in turn, invests beastliness with smallness. Thus, Osric serves to caricature the shortcomings of men more highly endowed in mind and character than he. At the same time, as a tool of men whose purposes he does not know, he demonstrates the predicament of the uninformed who elsewhere in the play serve the ends of evil. Like other young people with whom the bird images identify him, Osric is a pawn in a game that he does not even know is in progress; and his ignorance of the stakes is ironically underscored as he officiously details the wager and the arrangements of the "knightly" affair proposed by Claudius. Even Shakespeare's recurrent implication that there is something redeemable in every man is found in Osric's portrait and is perhaps thrown into sharper relief by Hamlet's contempt for this waterfly, chough, lapwing, beast: as umpire of the duel, he calls the touches fairly; he shows concern for Gertrude;

and no one, in Shakespeare's day, at least, would be likely to consider a regard for manner, custom, authority—to all of which Osric *intends* respect—as, in itself, undesirable.

Although Osric is absurd and Hamlet's remarks about him are sometimes rather more humorous than sardonic, irony keynotes the whole scene. Again, we see Hamlet contradict in action the spirit of the avowal that one should treat other men according to one's own dignity and honor, and thus put in question either his honesty or the dignity and honor that connives at such contempt. Again, we see him sitting in judgment on a fellow with no awareness that he censures himself. His scorn of Osric's business with hat and message recalls his determination to model his own action on Fortinbras's foray against the Poles, also a business he initially saw as vain and futile. The irony is compounded when (just after Osric leaves) Hamlet, deciding to duel with Laertes despite a sense of misgiving, says, "There's a special providence in the fall of a sparrow" (V.ii.230–31). He thus declares the place of all living creatures in a divine plan and, presumably, their consequence —an admirable philosophy. But characteristically, the biblical echo is employed when he thinks of himself and his own fate. He has been handing out bird labels to point to another man's inconsequence, ridiculing another man's high-flown speech and self-contradiction. Now he makes a noble speech about—of all things—God's concern in what happens to a bird. There is, of course, no necessary incompatibility in all this: but the easy and self-serving switch from pejorative bird-images to a declaration about the importance of a bird in the scheme of things smacks of his habitual inconsistency, his habitual resort to a noble speech directly at odds with his actions.

When Hamlet, in describing Osric as a "breed" the age dotes on and characterizing him in beast-figures, implies that the age dotes on the beast, he is criticizing the drossiness of the age and of the men it esteems. He is ridiculing not so much a regard for form, custom, and show, as the shape it takes. Yet, earlier, the Norman Lamond—who is held in the highest respect by society, who represents what Hamlet himself admires, and who is, ostensibly, the very opposite to the modish

Osric in *his* adherence to custom—is also subtly identified with a beast. Claudius praises the Norman:

> . . . he grew unto his seat;
> And to such wondrous doing brought his horse,
> As had he been incorpsed and demi-natured
> With the brave beast: so far he topp'd my thought,
> That I, in forgery of shapes and tricks,
> Come short of what he did.
> (IV.vii.86–91)

According to Claudius, Lamond's report of Laertes' skill with the rapier makes Hamlet wish to test himself against Laertes; thus, the reference to Lamond provides a history and an explanation for wager and challenge. But the passage goes beyond what plot requires. The account of Lamond's horsemanship and of Laertes' swordplay stresses the great esteem in which prowess in these knightly activities is held: Lamond is called "the brooch indeed / And gem of all the nation" (94–95); and his report of Laertes' art, which the "scrimers" of France could not match, "envenom[s]" Hamlet with envy—if we can believe Claudius. Proficiency in these skills—particularly in horsemanship, for which Claudius expresses a higher regard than for fencing and which he specifically assigns to the battlefield (84–85)—is useful in a "warlike state"; as skills, they are admirable in themselves. But Lamond, in whom a knightly art has reached a peak of excellence, appears therefore "demi-natured"; and whatever Claudius's intent, the description of Lamond has, in view of the overall pattern of beast imagery, implications reaching beyond the immediate context.

In a play where beast-figures repeatedly imply a departure from proper human nature, here is a man highly regarded because he seems half man, half horse. In a play where society exalts "antiquity [and] custom . . . / The ratifiers and props of every word" (IV.v.104–5) and ratifies and props a definition of honor by ancient custom, the "gem" of such a society has grown unto his seat and appears "incorpsed" with an animal. Despite Claudius's intention to invest Lamond with the bravery of the horse and thus enlarge a human excellence, figurative patterns throughout the play charge his words with pejorative meanings. The trapping imagery, to which we shall soon turn our attention, posits a relationship between entrapment in the form of a beast and a fall from human nature, a premise that accommodates the connotations of corruption in "incorpsed." Earlier, the "hellish" Pyrrhus is described as "couched in the ominous horse" (II.ii.485,476). The literal circumstance recalled in this allusion to the most famous of traps serves a pervasive figurative comment on the condition of the trapper, as well as the nature of trapping. And (in this play) *horse* is, if not ominous, charged by its connection with a show of some sort, with false appearance, or with inner disorder—whether Trojan horse, the "gift" that hides a murderous intent; hobbyhorse, the entertainer who, in accord with ancient custom, puts on the semblance of a beast; or jade galled by hidden guilt.

Thus, latent in the description of Lamond, extolled for a performance that the King says his "forgery" comes short of duly presenting, is the intimation that the Norman's "shapes and tricks" *are* defined by the forger. What is illustrated by Claudius's admiration is articulated by Hamlet in his disparagement of Osric: Claudius's praise links knightly custom and martial criteria with a man who is "demi-natured," and Hamlet's dispraise links false social values with admiration for a beastly man. When we hear a man who "grew unto" a beast lauded as the jewel of a nation and shortly thereafter that the "age dotes on" a beastly breed, we are struck less by the difference between two admired breeds than by the uniformity of the society that esteems them both; and we are led to question prevalent standards, whether embodied by Lamond and prefigured in his equestrian show or typified by Osric and imaged in his counterfeit courtliness. And when the epitome of knightly skills is said to be "incorpsed" and the exponent of current fashion is shown to be an ignorant medium for murder hidden in the guise of a knightly duel, we must infer that in "that monster, custom, who all sense doth eat," in blind adherence to form and inadequate ideal, may lie trap and death.

Less than a hundred lines after the description of the Nor-

man as "incorpsed and demi-natured / With the . . . beast"
comes a description of Ophelia as "mermaid-like" in the water,
"like a creature native and indued / Unto that element" (IV.
vii.177,180–81). Again, it may be argued that such lines are
mere picturesque embellishment. But, repeatedly, we have
found water and flood equated with evil, and beast imagery
defining the consequence of improper rule. The result of
"go[ing] to this water" and of having it "come to [the man]
and drown him," the role of wrong choice and of mischance—
both are aptly illustrated in the fate of Ophelia and in the
description of her as like a creature half maid, half fish. She
has chosen to mistrust Hamlet, later to allow Claudius and
the "fishmonger" Polonius to "loose" her so that they can bait
him; but she has been misled by a sense of duty, and she is
a victim of circumstance, as well as will. Such history is recalled in the account of her fall into the water and her drowning: we hear of a foolish "clambering" on a "pendant bough";
an accidental breaking of a "sliver"; an ambivalent effect from
garments that first "bore her up" but eventually "pull'd [her]
to muddy death" (167–84). And, appropriately, though the
image of the mermaid, along with those of the centaur and
the beastly breed of man, may hit hard, here near the end of
the play, at the result of an assent to misrule, "mermaid-like"
tips the scale toward a human rather than a beastly nature.
So, just prior to this, has Ophelia's speech in madness: it, too,
has reflected a demi-natured creature; but in her lewdness one
is led to find another demonstration of the pestilential nature
of evil, in such talk only the effect of her father's "contagious
blastments." That she is not a "creature . . . indued / Unto
that element" and that Claudius is not wholly right when he
says that she is "divided from herself and her fair judgement, /
Without the which we are . . . mere beasts" is revealed by
the prevailing truth and goodness in her speech even when
she is "distract."

In short, not only the transforming power of evil but the
degree of the individual assent to it, earlier projected in her
speech in madness, is imaged in "mermaid-like," as Shakespeare interweaves the strands of various figurative patterns
with the literal details of the death he assigns her. And whereas

the portraits of the demi-natured Lamond and Osric stress the immediate effect of either a lack of discrimination between values or a perversion of values, the description of the drowning Ophelia—while reiterating that beastliness and death may be, in part, the work of fortune and ignorance—also suggests that such consequences, given such causes, are not ultimate. The complex figurative interplay reinforces the general impression of Ophelia's character and leads us to doubt that Heaven's judgment accords with the judgment of a society that dotes on two young men it has victimized and denies the "mermaid-like" Ophelia burial in hallowed ground. Such conclusions are upheld by the comment in the trapping imagery, which we shall now consider, and from which grows a crucial general statement on a conduct common to all the principals of the play. Set over against it, in a counterpoint employing the same figurative referents, is an equally significant comment on another kind of conduct, one rarely found in *Hamlet*.

II

Frequently, those identified as beasts are also described as trapped or subject to trap. The "limed soul" of Claudius evokes a trap for birds; Polonius calls Hamlet's vows to Ophelia, "springes to catch woodcocks" (I.iii.115); Laertes, wounded by the sword he has anointed with a venom for Hamlet, says, "[I am] as a woodcock to mine own springe" (V.ii.317); Hamlet, who later identifies himself to Rosencrantz and Guildenstern as a fox, asks them, "Why do you go about to recover the wind of me, as if you would drive me into a toil?" (III.ii. 361–62); likening Gertrude to a beast who foolishly enters a trap, Hamlet says to her, "In despite of sense and secrecy, / Unpeg the basket on the house's top, / Let the birds fly, and, like the famous ape, / To try conclusions, in the basket creep" (III.iv.192–95). The characters describe themselves or others as hunters or fishers: Polonius "hunts . . . the trail of policy" (II.ii.47); Hamlet sees Claudius as a fisher who has "thrown out his angle for [Hamlet's] proper life" (V.ii.66); suggestively, even an invitation to a dramatic performance is expressed in terms of an indiscriminate hawking when Hamlet says, "We'll e'en to 't like French falconers, fly at any thing we see" (II.ii.449–50). The recurrent references to trap for the mouse, basket for ape and bird, springe and toil and angle for bird, animal, and fish, as well as to a predacious nature in the characters, forces the reader to reckon with the possibility of imminent trap for anyone identified in beast imagery. Thus, Hamlet's being greeted by the falconer's call to the hawk, "Hillo, ho, ho," just after he has talked with the Ghost, takes on an especial significance.

In short, the imagery suggests that in their treatment of their own kind, the various characters of the play have the beast in view and that those who partake of a beast nature are vulnerable to trap. Since both the trappers and the trapped men are described in beast images, beast eats beast in this "unweeded garden," and the closely interwoven pattern of image and event presents a twofold motif: the trapper trapped[14] and, conversely, the prey as predator. At the opening of the play, Francisco says in answer to whether he has had "quiet guard" (the appearance of the Ghost denotes unquiet guard), "Not a mouse stirring" (I.i.10). Then the mouse-Ghost appears and tells the story that, reenacted in the dumb show, "imports the argument" of "The Mouse-trap." The quarry of "The Mouse-trap" is the erstwhile mouser Claudius, who has also trapped the "mouse" Gertrude; and in reproducing Claudius's actions, Hamlet plays with him in cat-and-mouse fashion: the King watches a silent facsimile of his own trapping, not knowing whether it is trap or not, and is lured by seeming avenues of escape in Hamlet's observations on the play (III.ii.250–53). Not until Hamlet, imitating the poisoner, pours into the King's ears the argument of the play is Claudius sure of Hamlet's intent. And just as Claudius's own acts recoil upon him, so "The Mouse-trap" recoils upon Hamlet, whose death becomes the object of the King.

Trap-setting in *Hamlet* usually produces the same result; even if the outcome is not revealed, the character of the trapping, in its likeness to other inventions "fall'n on the inventors' heads," implies an inevitable rebound of the trap on the trapper. Polonius's method for enticing the "Danskers" in Paris into revealing the "truth" about Laertes is not unlike the method Hamlet employs in the dumb show and the play: Reynaldo is to present "forgeries" that, so Polonius argues, will elicit truths. And of Laertes, his father tells Reynaldo, "Observe his inclination" (II.i.71), as Hamlet tells Horatio, "Observe mine uncle" (III.ii.85). We do not learn the consequence of Polonius's scheme; but quite aside from its dishonorable nature, that such a practice could redound on Polonius in discrediting his son is obvious. Perhaps the teaching of a father who can justify the use of falsehood in the pursuit of honor is implicit in the means Laertes later employs to vindicate his honor: if so, when the "contagion" on the sword point "gall[s]" him (IV.vii.148), the infection in Polonius's speech returns on his own house. In a variation on the insistent figurative suggestion of the danger in speech, when Polonius places himself "in the ear / Of all [the] conference" between Hamlet and Gertrude (III.i.192–93), he finds the "ear" a vulnerable spot when Hamlet "speak[s] daggers" (III.ii.414). Polonius, like his son, may be killed by a weapon in Hamlet's hand; but he, too, invites his own destruction when he sets a mousetrap and is taken for a "rat."

Whether the pattern of recoil is illuminated by an imagery that identifies the victimizing speaker with the victim hearer or the beastly trapper with the trapped beast, the return of a destructive practice on the practitioner in a fitting measure is a leitmotif of the action: as the sword poisoned by Laertes kills him, so the drink poisoned by Claudius kills him and the wife whose welfare he cherishes. The pattern explicates the fate of Hamlet: aping madness to peg a basket for an ape, he is caught in his own springe, eventually unable to differentiate clearly between seeming and reality. And, similarly, since the Ghost does not want Gertrude "contriv[ed] against" or Hamlet's mind "taint[ed]," his vengefulness backfires. Even the lot of those who, desiring no man's death, still initiate or implement indirection contains variations, if in a minor key, on the theme that the punishment reflects the fault: Polonius, the exponent of the hidden and the roundabout procedure, finds the arras that obscures his true identity fatal; Rosencrantz and Guildenstern, trappers by proxy, become victims by proxy; Gertrude, won to a union with her husband's brother and accepting as "lawful" his and Polonius's use of Ophelia to spy on Hamlet (III.i.32), finds what lawlessness may accompany a "union" and a false practice when she drinks of the cup prepared for Hamlet; Ophelia, taught to mistrust, is mistrusted and, accessory to her father's first use of the arras, shares in the result of the second.

Thus, the motif of fitting recoil applies to all the victims. This statement, of course, requires considerable qualification, as does Hamlet's declaration about the deaths of Rosencrantz and Guildenstern, "Their defeat / Does by their own insinuation grow" (V.ii.58–59). Nevertheless, the fate of all of the principals may be, to some extent, clarified by the figurative and structural relationship between trapping and being trapped, between being mined and mining; by the workings of a pattern where a Ghost, in armor and prison-house, seeking a revenge that surely proves a bitter one, initiates a process wherein men, already limed by evil or brassed by "damned custom," are caught in traps they set for others. And this movement is precisely echoed in a mining imagery: the charge of the "old mole," a "worthy pioner" (I.v.163), starts the process where "the enginer [is] / Hoist with his own petar" (III.iv.206–7); and as the "worthy pioner" is himself already "blasted," so there is a recurrent implication that those who try to "blow [others] at the moon" are already infected by "corruption, mining all within" (209,148).

The error of all of the victims—if the beast-figures describing them are accurate—is generally defined in the passages where explicit distinctions are drawn between man and the beast. Claudius, as well as Hamlet, repeatedly expounds on this subject. Very early in the play, he calls Hamlet's excessive grief "unmanly": it shows improper rule, "a will most incorrect to heaven," and it is "to reason most absurd" (I.ii.94–95,103). Shortly thereafter, Hamlet invokes the same distinctions in implying that Gertrude's lack of grief falls short, not only of a human nature, but even of a beast nature: "a beast, that wants discourse of reason, / Would have mourn'd longer" (150–51). Later, in speeches that are again juxtaposed, Hamlet says:

FIGURATIVE DESIGN IN *HAMLET*

> What is a man,
> If his chief good and market of his time
> Be but to sleep and feed? a beast, no more.
> Sure, he that made us with such large discourse,
> Looking before and after, gave us not
> That capability and god-like reason
> To fust in us unused.
>
> (IV.iv.33–39);

and Claudius says, "Without ['fair judgement'] we are . . . mere beasts" (85–86).

God-like reason, proper rule, fair judgment: these distinguish a human from a beastly nature. Claudius's recognition of what raises man above the beast underscores the willfulness of his exercise of unreason when, for example, after lamenting his "heavy burthen" and declaring that his "wretched state" is the effect of sin (III.i.54;iii.66–67), he chooses to sin again. Laertes willfully rejects rule when he declares, "Conscience and grace, to the profoundest pit!" (IV.v.132). Whether sleeping and feeding were "the chief good and market" of King Hamlet's time, the words occur in descriptions of him, ironically by his greatest admirers: he is trapped sleeping, his "custom always of the afternoon" (I.v.59–60), and "full of bread" (III.iii.80), a phrase that recalls a biblical description of Sodom: "pride, fulness of bread, and abundance of idleness."[15] Gertrude, too, is described in a feeding imagery: "Why, she would hang on [King Hamlet], / As if increase of appetite had grown / By what it fed on," Hamlet says of her, and later to her, "Could you on this fair mountain [King Hamlet] leave to feed, / And batten on this moor [Claudius]?" (I.ii.143–45; III.iv.66–67). Such details support the traditional connotations in the mouse and mole figures and imply a fall from judgment and rule, although both of Hamlet's parents are equipped with such qualities (see, for example, I.v.27 and II.ii.95). And however much some of Hamlet's admirers may boggle at the suggestion that he can be beastly, by his own definition he can be so labeled. When, for example, he muses on Fortinbras's march against the Poles and cites "discourse" and reason as human attributes denied the beast, he is shown in one of his most startling displays of unreason. His reason tells him that the Poles will never defend a worthless "little patch of ground"; that lives and wealth are vainly expended on a trifling matter; that the whole action is "the imposthume of much wealth and peace, / That inward breaks, and shows no cause without / Why the man dies" (IV.iv.23,25–29). But after thus criticizing Fortinbras's action, he turns about and, as if it were a touchstone to excellence, declares, "How all occasions do inform against me"; after saying that God does not give men "reason / To fust in [them] unused," he takes the stand that Fortinbras's action, which he has found unreasonable, must be his model. First, he says that men must be led by "god-like reason"; then, by "examples gross as earth." Ironically, Shakespeare shows him philosophizing on the advantages of the human gifts of discourse and reason, then discoursing and reasoning that the praiseworthy way to settle differences is physical combat—what any beast is capable of. The stirring sound of Hamlet's words should not mislead the reader: he is unreasonable in the very speech that extols reason; changing color like the chameleon he earlier likens himself to, he glorifies what he has just labeled an "imposthume."

Here Shakespeare gives us a pointed illustration of the error that Hamlet has just warned Gertrude against: reason pandering will (III.iv.88). And this is a fault common to characters in other ways dissimilar. "Reason pandars will" in the Ghost's slant description of himself (I.v.55), despite the realities of his state; and in Polonius's telling Reynaldo to accuse Laertes of gaming, drinking, swearing, quarreling, drabbing, but not to say anything that will dishonor him, rather to "breathe his faults so quaintly" that they may seem "the taints of liberty" (II.i.24–32).[16] And though Claudius, who sees good clearly and chooses evil deliberately, does not casuistically call evil good, he does call it *his* good when he names the death of Hamlet his "cure" (IV.iii.67–69). Since he elsewhere admits that one murder has brought him sickness, the declaration that another will bring him health shows reason pandering will, as when Milton's Satan, despite his admission that to be greatest in evil is to be most miserable, cries, "Evil be thou my good."

If a departure from reason, rule, and judgment defines a fall from proper human nature, it is not difficult to establish the appropriateness of the beast labels for all the principals. But though it may be second nature to Polonius to pervert reason to serve the ends of self, rather than himself serving the ends of reason; though Gertrude's hasty remarriage may reflect a lack of rule and judgment and the feeding imagery describing her recall the "chief good and market" of the beast; though it might be argued that Ophelia is ill-judging to put her faith in her father's words, instead of Hamlet's, and even that Rosencrantz and Guildenstern too thoughtlessly assume that authority is not to be questioned, still such error is qualified by an absence of ill will and a lack of knowledge. Polonius wants no man's death; Gertrude, Ophelia, Rosencrantz and Guildenstern are like the little eyases: they are not the authors of destructive plots against their fellows. But Hamlet foresees the recoil of the action of the little eyases on themselves when they are adult performers; and if, as the figurative pattern imports, the consequence suggests a voluntary wrongdoing, then even those who are unwitting tools of men with murderous intents may be, if trapped, identified in some sense as trappers. For essentially, the idea behind the peculiar demonstrations in *Hamlet* of a man's being "hoist with his own petar" seems to be as uncompromising as "The wages of sin is death," a prediction that does not differentiate between sins.

A purpose and a fault that those who do not want any man's death share with those who do are a search for truth and a willingness to deal in untruth. Shakespeare takes pains to point to the inaccurate reporting of fact in the court, not just to the difference in the eyes of the beholders by which he suggests the difficulty of arriving at truth,[17] but to the willful misrepresentation and the almost mechanical deceit that by its very needlessness reveals the pernicious climate of a country wherein there is a fallout of falsehood. Polonius, who counsels, "To thine own self be true, / And it must follow, as the night the day / Thou canst not then be false to any man" (I.iii.78–80), exemplifies the prevalent discipleship to self. The inconsequence of his misleading account to Claudius and Gertrude of his reason for telling Ophelia to avoid Hamlet's company[18] attests to the self-corruption that attends a relative standard of conduct. And his daughter, on one occasion at least, proves native to the element of equivocation, which is as natural as water in Denmark: her words to Hamlet when she "re-delivers" his gifts—"to the noble mind / Rich gifts wax poor when givers prove unkind" (III.i.100–101)—unfairly load the scales in her own favor. A claim to the "noble mind," while unjustly putting all the blame for her action on the unkindness of Hamlet, directs us to sympathize with his re-action, "Ha, ha! are you honest?" Gertrude, after agreeing not to inform the King that Hamlet "essentially [is] not in madness" (III.iv.187), goes a long step further and says that he is mad (IV.i.7); and just after she hears Hamlet remark on Polonius's dead body with "I'll lug the guts into the neighbour room" (III.iv.212), she reports that he weeps over Polonius's death. If so, her interpretation of the weeping (IV.i. 25–27) misrepresents what she and we have seen and heard. Even in a play where the danger in false-seeming is insistently emphasized, one might be led to make allowance for a mother's protective instincts; but what strikes one about Gertrude's untruths is that they are essentially needless. As for Rosencrantz and Guildenstern, latest come to court and least tainted by the prevailing climate, they are led, by the nature of their employment, to an equivocation that, though transient, contains the seed of their destruction. "What's the news?" says Hamlet at their arrival in Elsinore; and Rosencrantz answers, "None, my lord, but that the world's grown honest" (II.ii. 240–42). Being the stuff of inconsequential talk, perhaps this remark should not be "set in a note-book . . . To cast into [the speaker's] teeth"[19] when he later tells of the use made of the child players in a "nation [that] holds it no sin to tarre [people] to controversy" (370). But a characteristically Shakespearean irony marks an assertion that "the world's grown honest" by a speaker who is dodging the import of a question. When Hamlet replies that the "news is not true" and, questioning "more in particular," asks why they are come to court, both of his friends avoid answering; again he asks, and again Rosencrantz equivocates, "To visit you, my lord; no other occasion" (279); four times more he repeats the question in various forms, and they continue to hedge. It is not until he says, "If you love me, hold not off" that Guildenstern answers directly, "My lord, we were sent for" (301–3). The awkwardness of their evasions suggests that neither is an experienced dissembler and that when Hamlet says that they have "a kind of confession in [their] looks which [their] modesties have not craft enough to colour" (288–90), he describes them more truly than later when he implies that they are liars (III.ii.372) and invests them with the craft of "adders" (III.iv.203). And though Rosencrantz's report to the King that Hamlet has been "niggard of question; but, of our demands, / Most free in his reply" (III.i.13–14)[20] is not precisely in line with Guildenstern's "Nor do we find him forward to be sounded, / But, with a crafty madness, keeps aloof, / When we would bring him on to some confession / Of his true state" (7–10), the reading that recommends itself for all of the speeches of both men, after their initial essay at a dissembling unnatural to them, is that they say what they believe. But the fact that they are not, at first, straightforward with Hamlet evokes his mistrust; and such reaction (like his mistrust of Ophelia), if growing out of all proportion, serves to illustrate the boomerang of the equivocating speech or act.

If one asks what springs the trap for the fox Hamlet, the bat Claudius, the rat Polonius, the mouse Gertrude, the woodcocks Ophelia and Laertes, even the "hernshaws" Rosencrantz and Guildenstern, one does not ask only what baits them, but also what bait they use, since according to the pattern of recoil, all are, to some extent, self-destroyed. Polonius says, "Your bait of falsehood takes this carp of truth" (II.i.63); but obviously the "carp" that the "buzzer" and "fishmonger" brings to market is not truth. Yet all of the trappers (and their tools) hold to Polonius's philosophy: all try "by indirections [to] find directions out" (66). When the King and Polonius put into effect the latter's plan to "loose [his] daughter" to Hamlet (II.ii.162) so that they may determine the nature of Hamlet's "madness," Ophelia is an accomplice in the matter and, at her father's bidding, adopts a "show" to

"colour [her] loneliness" (III.i.45–46). Gertrude, also privy
to this trapping, without protest accepts the method of the
King and Polonius; later, not objecting to the "craft" that
Hamlet admits to practicing on Claudius (III.iv.188), she
again becomes accessory to whatever false-seeming may lead
to. Laertes, under the King's tutelage, sets the "bait of falsehood" in inviting Hamlet to what purports to be a contest
of skill. And Rosencrantz and Guildenstern, though knowing
nothing of the King's plot to have Hamlet killed in England,
are (like Ophelia) caught by a manifestation of a method
they earlier countenance. What springs the trap for all is their
own acceptance of untruth: setting the "bait of falsehood,"
they are trapped by "indirections." If such an argument (that
entrapment in *Hamlet* posits a willful connivance at trapping
and that the fate of all elaborates on the self-destruction in
the use of false-seeming) appears untenable, since the consequence may be out of proportion to the offense or does not
properly discriminate between the small offender and the
great, one is forgetting the significance of such lines as "Above
. . . the action lies / In his true nature" (III.iii.60–62) and
incorrectly inferring from the argument that only physical
destruction defines and punishes error.

The comment we have been tracing in the beast-trap imagery on the nature and effect of sin, joined to an invocation
to proper action, the antithesis to setting the "bait of falsehood," appears in words spoken by the mad Ophelia: "They
say the owl was a baker's daughter. Lord, we know what we
are, but know not what we may be. God be at your table!" (IV.
v.41–43). The old legend illustrates again the sinner's beastliness and entrapment: the baker's daughter, who refuses to
give bread to Christ, is changed into an owl; her lack of humanity makes her subject to trap, and her nature is crystallized
when she is "incorpsed" in the form of a beast. And the
figurative likeness between her and the victims in *Hamlet*
identifies their failing with hers and points to the alternative
action they, too, neglected: to give bread to Christ, to have
God at their table. "Conceit upon her father," explains Claudius when he hears Ophelia say the latter words; and indeed it
is, but not upon the chamberlain Polonius, whom the King has

in mind. Shakespeare's conceit is subtly operating in Claudius's explanation, as Ophelia's later words suggest: "It is the false steward, that stole his master's daughter" (172–73). In a drama that concerns the duty and honor owed to earthly fathers, we are reminded at various times and in various ways —this is one of them—that a prior duty and honor is owed to a heavenly father and that an offense against him (against Truth, Reason, Order) is incompatible with a proper discharge of one's duties to or as an earthly father. Such allusions as those to the baker's daughter who refused to give bread to Christ and to the false steward who stole his master's daughter evoke the theological commonplace that man's health and freedom are ultimately dependent on the Food and the Word.

By its very nature, an exposition of a complex figurative pattern may invest the most subtle play of image and idea with its own heavyhandedness; but though such language as the Food and the Word may not seem appropriate to Shakespeare, the concept in the words is essentially what his fancy is manipulating. We are reminded by these allusions, not only that the chamberlain's daughter, who refuses to trust in Hamlet's "holy vows," eventually becomes mad and like one "deminatured" and that the chamberlain, serving the "bait of falsehood," turns "God's creature" into bait, but also that bait and falsehood, rather than bread and truth, are the prevalent forms of exchange in Denmark. A beastly feeding is the "market of [the] time," whether the beast feeds on the mountain or battens on the moor, or in other ways gobbles up his own kind. Hamlet's comment on the worm that eats of a king, the fish that eats of the worm, the beggar that eats of the fish, so that "a king [goes] a progress through the guts of a beggar" (IV.iii.28–33) is the process in this world where beast eats beast, where "fat king and . . . lean beggar is but variable service, two dishes, but to one table" (24–25). In a court where men do not have God at their table, they feed on one another in a cannibalistic free-for-all and "fat [themselves] for maggots."

Though the trappers in *Hamlet* think that falsehood can catch truth, Polonius's description of truth as "this carp" connotes that the nature of the catch is appropriate to the method: those who "angle" catch something that, in this play, moves in an element of evil. And the figurative implications are borne out in the dramatic action as the trappers and fishers, rejecting the Word for falsehood and the Food for bait, failing to give bread to Christ and to have God at their table, invite self-destruction: metaphorical design and literal event insistently echo and reecho the predications that the man who sets in motion the sound of evil is bound to bear its reverberations and that the man who baits others baits himself.

III

Sidney Warhaft says, "When we think of King Hamlet's 'foul crimes' done in his 'days of nature' we are confronted with . . . fantastic possibilities. Had things perhaps begun to decline to their confounding contraries *before* Claudius dispatched his brother?"[21] According to the figurative comment, the condition envisioned in this question is more than possibility and less than fantastic. Indeed, behind the immediate circumstances and also behind events taking place in the lifetime of King Hamlet is a garden where the father of falsehood, incorpsed in the form of a beast, poisons the ears of Eve and baits her with an apple. The poison-ear imagery, the confinement and beast-trap imagery, the process of self-destruction as the victims are tempted and defeated by the "bait of falsehood," recall a start for "confounding contraries" long before Claudius reenacts the role of the serpent in the garden and the others imitate Satan insofar as they put on the nature of the beast. *Hamlet* is played out against a backdrop of the Fall. If one shies a bit at Kitto's declaration that in this play "the Tragic Hero, ultimately, is humanity itself," one must concede that the figurative comment supports the rest of his sentence, "and what humanity is suffering from . . . is not a specific evil, but Evil itself."[22]

This is not to deny the obvious: evil takes on specific forms in *Hamlet*, and its prime early manifestation is the murder of King Hamlet, a catalyst that looses a flood of evil on Denmark. But the large perspective afforded by the metaphorical design must qualify our opinion of Hamlet's view that all of the corruption in Denmark emanates from Claudius, as our knowledge of all that Shakespeare says, not just what he says by way of Hamlet, must qualify an adoption of Hamlet's opinions. Those critics who take Hamlet for their moral interpreter must also accept a "moral interpretation" by any character echoing Hamlet's convictions, no matter how questionable Shakespeare's manipulation of incident reveals it to be. "The king, the king's to blame," cries Laertes (V.ii.331) when he and Hamlet are wounded by the poisoned sword, the baiting of which is not the King's idea but Laertes' own elaboration of the plot. And critics who show no charity when Laertes is the object of their criticism take up the refrain when they focus on Claudius. Yet Laertes—willing to "dare damnation" before the King proposes the duel, admitting to Osric that he is caught in his own springe and to Hamlet that the "foul practice" has "turn'd itself" on him—sums up the whole matter on a familiar note that sounds ironically throughout the play: "The king's to blame." There is, of course, truth in Laertes' words, but such abridgment is neither consistent nor accurate, surely a significant fact here at the end of the play and one reinforcing an ambivalence in the accusation not intended by the accuser. The technique is one that Shakespeare employs repeatedly: the report not quite in line with what we have seen; the words contradicted by the speaker's actions or by other words of his; the description contrary to what we see and hear. "Most generous and free from all contriving" is Claudius's description of Hamlet (IV.vii.136) after the presentation of "The Mouse-trap" has convinced him that Hamlet is dangerous and shortly before we hear Hamlet's account of his cruel contrivance against Rosencrantz and Guildenstern. "A very noble youth" is Hamlet's description of Laertes (V.i.247) not long after we see Laertes plotting treachery and murder and just before Hamlet's contemptuous use of dog and cat images to describe him.

Shakespeare does not employ this technique to encourage us to accept any one character's description or opinion of another; and certainly the import of the figurative pattern, as well as a process described in it, pointedly warns us against heeding only the persuasive rhetoric that Hamlet pours into our ears. Nevertheless, critical judgments of all the characters sometimes rely only on Hamlet's words or some of his words. It has been said that Claudius "had a small nature,"[23] an estimate that picks up Hamlet's contempt for his uncle, but not his description, "mighty opposite," and that discounts the evidence of Claudius's courage, strength, intelligence, administrative wisdom and diplomacy, dignity, and charm. To grant Claudius admirable qualities is not to sentimentalize over him any more than over Satan when one accepts a seventeenth-century estimate of him as the Adversary "in courage most hardie, in strength most mightie, in policies most subtle, in diligence unweariable." The corruption of the "noble substance," which engages Hamlet's attention in his brief definition of tragedy, is a basic subject of the play. And in Claudius, as in Milton's Satan, the glimpses of ruined virtue measure the destructiveness of sin and the extent of corruption. To argue that Claudius is "small" in nature is not only to disregard the workings of a fundamental theme but to minimize Hamlet's problem and to cheapen the whole tragic effect. On the other hand, whatever one may say of Claudius's flashes of honesty, his pangs of conscience, the surface order of his rule, his courtesy or tact or concern for his subjects, to declare that he represents health and normality and Hamlet sickness and abnormality (on the basis of any level for argument) is to turn the play topsy-turvy and to ignore the theme that an evil deed unrepented brings on a continual ruining from good. Claudius may have noble attributes, and so long as he is top dog, his own will not opposed, he may display the better side of his nature; but he is also a "bloody . . . treacherous . . . kindless villain" (II.ii.608–9). And if one claims that his evil does not excuse Hamlet's, one certainly cannot say that Hamlet's action relieves Claudius of blame. G. Wilson Knight says, "We can say . . . that [Hamlet's] faults . . . are forced on him by a bad society . . . and therefore [are] not properly faults. Yet from that standpoint we can say as much for many wrongdoers. . . . we must surely see guilt in Hamlet's behaviour." But of Claudius he says, "Granted the fact of his original crime which cannot now be altered, Claudius can hardly be blamed for his later actions. They are forced on him."[24] Quite aside from whether Shakespeare would flirt with such an idea before rejecting it or whether he would espouse it, Professor Knight does both; and self-contradiction is almost inevitable if one takes a short view of this play. Shakespeare directs our gaze far back in time: the error in drawing an arbitrary line and finding a start for "confounding contraries" in Claudius's crime may be glimpsed in the more obvious error of starting with Hamlet's reaction to that crime.

If a view afforded by a figurative pattern that sets the action of all the victims in relief against the largest of backgrounds and projects in all a common failing leads us to qualify Hamlet's opinion of Claudius, it does not invalidate the truth in that opinion. But the narrowness of his view of other characters is a crucial matter, for it diminishes him in a way that his view of Claudius does not. The fate of all the victims may reflect the theme, "If the man go to this water, and drown himself, it is, will he, nill he, he goes"; but some of these "drownings" may also illustrate the accompanying theme, "If the water come to him and drown him, he drowns not himself: argal, he that is not guilty of his own death shortens not his own life." Only the first of these applies to Claudius: the reprisal that comes to him is inherent in his own act; he "shortens . . . his own life" when he kills his brother; he exemplifies the figurative truth in the Clown's claim that "your water is a sore decayer of your whoreson dead body" (V.i.189–90) and, drowned, is "rotten before he die[s]" (180). But both themes apply to Rosencrantz and Guildenstern: they voluntarily practice equivocation, but they are also victim to Hamlet's disproportionate falsehood. Perhaps more than any other characters they serve as sounding boards for the change in Hamlet.[25] His estimates of them—from the time when he says that they lack "craft" to the time when he applies to them the snake-image, which the Ghost uses for Claudius—reflect his narrowing perception of reality.

His first greeting of the "good lads," as he calls them (II.ii. 229), leads us to believe that Rosencrantz's later remark, "My lord, you once did love me" (III.ii.348) is true. They do not understand his altering manner toward them, but surely we are meant to realize that their allegiance to Claudius and their early lack of candor to Hamlet (like Ophelia's seeming fickleness) occur at a time when such conduct assumes for Hamlet an importance out of all measure to its weight. Unlike Hamlet, we hear the explanation they are given for their employment—that the King wants to "remedy" whatever "afflicts" Hamlet; Guildenstern's response, "Heavens make our presence and our practices / Pleasant and helpful to him!" (II.ii.17–18,38–39); and their later innocuous report to the King. We know that they, unlike Horatio after Hamlet's departure for England, are in attendance on a ruler whose authority they have no reason to question. We know that, aside from Ophelia, they alone among the victims apply no abusive epithets to anyone in Elsinore. We see Guildenstern, unlike Osric and Polonius, rebuke Hamlet with dignity for his rudeness: "This courtesy is not of the right *breed*. If it shall please you to make me a wholesome answer, I will do your mother's commandment: if not, your pardon and my return shall be the end of my business" (III.ii.326–30, italics mine). We are surely meant to notice the incongruity of Hamlet's picking Guildenstern for the object of his pipe-playing analogy; he accuses Guildenstern of trying to "play upon" him, of trying to "sound [him] from [his] lowest note to the top of [his] compass" (380–83) when his former schoolfellow says only that the King is angry and that the Queen has sent him to Hamlet with a message. It is Rosencrantz who questions Hamlet; and, after his early clumsy attempt at indirection, he is direct: "Good my lord, what is your cause of distemper?" (350), a question that, from *his* point of view, is hardly an attempt to "drive [Hamlet] into a toil" (362). What we see of the actions of the two men recommends Hamlet's first words about them—good lads, lacking in craft—rather than his later varying ones—adders, sponges, fools—or the names some critics give them—toadies, yes-men, time-servers. The details of their murder place them in the class of the wronged victim King Hamlet, and their murderer in the category of Claudius. Like the former King, they are connived against while sleeping; but the "market of [the beast's] time" that informs the King's "custom" of sleeping "always of the afternoon" does not apply to them, although the circumstance is suggestive of their nature and of their unknowing, unwary sojourn in a land that is not "grown honest." Like the former King, they are sent to their death "unhousel'd"; but again there is a difference. The King dies "full of bread," and the biblical echoes distinguish this "bread" from the "food" that he is denied by his killer. But nothing in what we are told of Hamlet's victims suggests that their lack of the Eucharist could be reflected in such a reaction as that of the Ghost; that their physical death is not the end of their trial and payment for error; that they will be "doom'd for a certain term to walk the night"; or that, if Hamlet had lived, their ghosts would return for revenge. The implications in the beast-trap imagery that the ultimate consequence of their error is far different from that to which Claudius's evil-doing brings him point to the moral blindness in the man who kills them all. Hamlet's dispatching of Rosencrantz and Guildenstern measures his own departure from reality, a matter to be dealt with in the following discussion of the *show* symbolism.

CHAPTER SIX

I

We have seen that insofar as the traditional nature of the dumb show helps to inform a complex figurative pattern, Shakespeare is using the stage as a touchstone, as well as a means, to a comment on the nature of evil, of false-seeming. But we have not canvassed the variety of a method that "hold[s] . . . the mirror up to nature" by setting up a glass to the stage. We have not, for example, traced in any detail the instances where the Danes are characterized by way of explicit references to their correspondence to stage figures whose reality or unreality is a matter of explicit question. So before considering the large import of the show and the play symbolism, I should like to document certain comparisons supporting the proposition that Shakespeare uses the stage as a reagent to measure the substance of *being*.

Repeatedly, the characters in *Hamlet* identify themselves or their fellows with characters in a drama; and obviously comparisons between two arenas of dramatic action may serve a purpose that the speaker cannot envisage. We know that Hamlet associates the principals in the dumb show (the Player King, the Player Queen, and the Poisoner) and in the following playlet (Gonzago, Baptista, and Lucianus) with King Hamlet, Gertrude, and Claudius; that he uses drama to jolt

Claudius into revealing a recognition of his own likeness to the Poisoner/Lucianus. We cannot know that when he describes Lucianus as "nephew to the king," he deliberately employs the word *king* instead of *duke* in a veiled threat to Claudius and, intimating a Lucianus/Hamlet likeness, consciously shifts the analogy. The logic of the play-scene and the character of Gonzago make it unlikely that Hamlet sees himself in Gonzago's killer. Yet if we judge by Hamlet's importunate speech to Lucianus (III.ii.262–65), the latter is (like Hamlet) portrayed as one who puts on "faces" and puts off homicide, and who is urged, in the name of revenge, to act.

Again, we can reasonably infer that Hamlet sees in the principals in the Player's Speech (Priam, Hecuba, and Pyrrhus) his father, mother, and uncle; that the performance he requests may serve a need to project his own grief and horror at his father's death, his desire to see his mother react to that death with a "burst of clamour" (II.ii.538), his hate for Claudius—perhaps a need to strengthen his resolution by a vivid account of the slaying of a king and father. But it is unlikely that, in calling for this particular speech, he has in mind a detail omitted in the speech—that Pyrrhus is a son with a dear father slain—or that he recalls, from his previous knowledge of the speech, similarities between himself and an avenger who is clothed in black; whose sword "seem[s] i' the air to stick"; and who, purposing vengeance, "like a neutral to his will and matter, [does] nothing" (501–4). The fact that Pyrrhus is the villain of the piece; the descriptions of him as "beast" and "tyrant," words used elsewhere to describe Claudius; Hamlet's subsequent view of his own "cue for passion" in the light of the Player's cue (which is certainly not the justice of Pyrrhus's cause)—all this gainsays a conclusion that Hamlet consciously sees himself in Priam's killer.

If Hamlet is not aware of likenesses that we are led to recognize, then Shakespeare is employing the dramatic insets for purposes that include, but also extend beyond, Hamlet's own purposes. Even if we concede Hamlet the most remarkable ambivalence of feeling and perception in his awareness of analogies afforded by the inner-stage description or action, he cannot take into account all of the ironies available to us in a court performance that projects similarities between Lucianus and both Claudius and Hamlet, or in a speech that accommodates comparisons between Pyrrhus and both Claudius and Hamlet. Hamlet's vantage point is not that of the *Hamlet* audience, which is privy to words and actions in Denmark of which Hamlet knows nothing. Moreover, Shakespeare's use of correspondences between what is, to Hamlet, actuality and what is, to him, representation—"a fiction . . . a dream"—must range beyond Hamlet's awareness and use of those correspondences, since Hamlet himself is a character in a drama.

The very frequency of instances where *Hamlet* characters identify themselves or others with figures on a stage suggests that the associations serve a larger purpose than that intended by the speaker or found in the immediate context of the speech. For example, Ophelia likens Hamlet to "a chorus" (III.ii.255); he identifies the "dallying" of her and her lover with that of "puppets" in a play (256–57); he compares the forgetting of a "great man" in his real world of Denmark with the forgetting of a character in certain Whitsun entertainments, the outmoded hobbyhorse who, concealing his human legs in trappings, gives an imitation of a beast (139–45); he calls the spectators in the last scene "mutes" (V.ii.346). And the action of the Danes is repeatedly described in a terminology of theater: the mute appearance of the Ghost and the speech of the mad Ophelia, who deals in "winks, and nods, and gestures," are (like the uninformative jingle preceding "The Mouse-trap") linked with "prologue" (I.i.123;IV.v.11,18); theatrical prologue is conjured up when Gertrude says, "What act, / That roars so loud, and thunders in the index?" (III. iv.51–52), and explicitly recalled when Hamlet, telling Horatio of his forgery of Claudius's letter to England, says, "Ere I could make a prologue to my brains, / They had begun the play" (V.ii.30–31); Hamlet implies a likeness between Ophelia's "show" and the action of the players in the dumb show (III.ii.154–55), and shortly before he makes this comparison, the word "show" is used to describe Ophelia's action as staged by Polonius and Claudius (III.i.45); after the latter are hidden audience to this "show," Polonius uses the word "audience" to describe his "vantage" in the Queen's closet (III.

iii.31); and the spectators of the scene of general violence at the close of the play are called "audience to [an] act" (V.ii.345). Of course, such words may carry a general meaning; nevertheless, they also keep one in mind of theater. The list of such instances could be greatly extended (and I shall shortly have occasion to add to it); but these examples demonstrate that the identification of the Danes with stage characters, performers, or audience is not limited to connections afforded by the dramatic insets. So although Hamlet may use similarities between events in Denmark and Vienna to expedite his plot, Shakespeare has more than mere plot in mind when the action of characters on whose lifelikeness he expends great art is echoed by bloodless figures on an inner stage.

One product, often noted by critics, of the use of two *stages* is a perspective on two kinds of theater. The *Hamlet* characters have a life of their own; those in the dumb show and *Gonzago* are puppets, stagy representatives of nature once removed. Language and action in the dramatic inset—the stiffness, the formality, the ceremony, the whole effect of superficial show—contrast with the framing matter. Thus, by a difference between two kinds of seeming—the stage world of Vienna and the stage world of Denmark—Shakespeare draws distinctions between dramatic unreality and dramatic reality. A by-product, one not noted by critics, of the presence of two *audiences* is that we are invited to view the *Hamlet* characters by way of their view of stage characters. "What's Hecuba to him, or he to Hecuba, / That he should weep for her?" says Hamlet of the First Player (II.ii.585–86). From our vantage point, we might say, "What's Hamlet to us, or we to Hamlet, / That we should weep for him?" Thus, by a line between the world of the play and the world of the audience— the "unreal" Carthage and the "real" Denmark—Shakespeare gives the definitions of unreality and reality another dimension. And Hamlet's distinctions between his real and his representational worlds parallel our reality as audience and his unreality as stage figure. Yet, any definition effected by the line between the worlds of the Danish audience and their stage is modified by the fact that the Danish audience *un-*

knowingly occupy a stage, a matter that has implications for the audience of *Hamlet*.

Moreover, distinctions between domains of stage and audience are further complicated by the peculiar nature of a dramatic rendering of "Aeneas' tale to Dido," which explicitly establishes an audience, albeit unseen, within the dramatic frame. The result is that Shakespeare's audience in, say, London watches an audience in Elsinore watching a dramatic portrayal of Aeneas telling an audience in Carthage what happened in Troy and what the spectator of such a sight must have felt. Whereas in the dumb show we only see what later in *Gonzago* we both "hear and see" (III.i.23), the First Player's Speech projects an audience we neither see nor hear; yet as we supplement unheard speech in the dumb show, we imagine the unseen hearer of Aeneas's tale. The Player enacts what happens in Carthage, and though the words direct our gaze to Troy, it is impossible to divorce the speech from the histories of the speaker Aeneas and the hearer Dido. Resultant associations between various times and places and between the deaths of various kings, fathers, and husbands, reinforce the implication we have noted elsewhere that we are to view the happenings in Denmark against a long historical perspective. But the most noteworthy aspect of a dramaturgic tour de force that entails a mute, unseen presence is the shifting estate of the real and the representational: to Dido, Aeneas's tale presents facts that have a counterpart in facts in her own life; to Hamlet, that same tale is fiction resembling facts in his life; to Shakespeare's audience, fiction echoes fiction.

Just what literary recollections Shakespeare intends to elicit in his version of a part of Aeneas's tale to Dido is, of course, debatable.[1] But we can reasonably suppose that a seventeenth-century audience could hardly avoid supplementing it with some details from the lives of both speaker and hearer: Aeneas, who bewails the killing of a king and father,[2] is noted for his patriotism and filial devotion; Dido, who is told of the grief of a bereaved wife, has suffered a husband's murder[3] and is to commit suicide at the loss of Aeneas. If the horror of the speaker Aeneas at a lack of pity for a "reverend sire" is duplicated in Denmark, so is the inconsistency of that speaker who can later kill a prince, despite the latter's plea for pity in the name of a father's grief.[4] And if the previous experience of the hearer Dido with such acts and feelings as those described in the tale (as well as with a ghost's return to tell of a secret murder) finds counterparts in Denmark, so does the later tragedy of that hearer who is to invite her own death.

In short, behind events in Elsinore the Player's Speech hangs a backdrop of Carthage, Tyre, and Latium, as well as Troy. And the speech accommodates a variety of comparisons: parallels between Hecuba, Dido, and Gertrude; similarities between their husbands Priam, Sychaeus, and Hamlet Senior, and between their husbands' killers, the tyrants Pyrrhus, Pygmalion, and Claudius; ironic and complex correspondences between Pyrrhus, Aeneas, Dido, and Hamlet, all revenge-seekers; subtle equivalences between Hamlet and both the speaker Aeneas and the hearer Dido. This is not to say that the *Hamlet* audience could be expected to perceive and sort out all of these connections as he hears the Player's Speech: I present no brief for the need to do so; nor do I insist that any comparison I suggest here is unexceptionable. Manifest in the matter and context of the speech itself are certain iterations in attitude or experience between characters on the outer stage, on the inner stage, and in the tale; manifest is the repetitiveness of history, "whose common theme" is violence and grief. But a comparative study of the Player's Speech, its counterpart in the *Aeneid,* and other events in the lives of Aeneas and Dido does suggest a reason for Shakespeare's selection of this particular account of a king's murder: that an evocation of analogy is here especially purposeful and significant. What is reality in Carthage to Dido is seeming to Hamlet in Elsinore; and what is reality to Hamlet is seeming to us: the definition of the real and the representational, of fact and fiction, depends on the eye of the beholder. Yet the analogies between characters in different times and places underscore the relativity, the inadequacy, of such a definition.

Immediately after the Player's Speech, Hamlet comments

indirectly on reality and unreality; his referent is the dramatic performance he has just witnessed, and the imprecision of the observations that Shakespeare gives him is surely calculated to arouse our attention. When he says of the Player, "What's Hecuba to him . . . ?" he evokes the factual dissociation between the Player and Hecuba. Insofar as the Player fails to project the dramatic reality (and his hearers appear to be uncomfortably aware of him, rather than Aeneas), insofar as he loses control and, weeping in his own person, is a player in Denmark, rather than Aeneas in Carthage, Hamlet's focus on him is understandable. Nevertheless, properly speaking, Aeneas weeps, and Hecuba is something to Aeneas. Hamlet disregards the distinction between the Player and the play role; and his narrow insistence on the Player's removal in time and place from the tragedy he laments, fails to take into account the purpose of playing. On a slightly different score, we take issue with the assumption in the question. Whether or not the Player succeeds in making Aeneas's grief real to his audience, all indications are that it is real to him. There *is* a reality that transcends the apprehensions of the senses, a reality Hamlet neglects in his differentiation between a "fiction" and present fact, between the world of the stage and the world of the audience.

Moreover, he compounds his disregard for the nature and the purpose of playing when he goes on to say of the Player, "What would he do, / Had he the motive and the cue for passion / That I have? He would drown the stage with tears" (II.ii.586–88). It might be argued that Hamlet intends to contrast his cause for grief with that of Aeneas, to say that if the Player were projecting Hamlet's "cue for passion" instead of Aeneas's, he would have a subject of greater and more immediate tragic import to work with. But the logic (or illogic) of the whole passage makes such an inference debatable. Since he has been focusing on the Player's (not Aeneas's) grief over the murder of a father, we must suppose that he is still separating the Player from any *play* role: if the Player could weep so for someone he never knew, he would, given a personal motive, "drown the stage with tears." And the tenor of the passage suggests that the greater "motive . . . for passion" that Hamlet envisions for the **Player** is the murder of the Player's father.

We may concede that insofar as Hamlet and the Player occupy the same arena of action—that is, Denmark, not the Danish stage—the long-past murder of a stranger does not afford a "cue for passion" so great as the present murder of a father. But an actor's motive cannot be equated with that of a person not on the stage; obviously, even if an actor were to present an autobiographical matter on the stage, his motive would not be the one that had operated in an organic and unfinished offstage action. And when Hamlet appears to move from defining the action of the stage as "fiction" to suggesting that the action of one's own life could be removed to the stage without undergoing any alteration in motive, we question his conception of reality, dramatic or otherwise. Quite aside from the turn given his remarks by the fact that we hear them through the medium of an actor, we wonder at even the slightest intimation that a bereaved son would choose to express his reaction to injury and loss on a stage; at the implication that such action would add up to an emotion in stage fare not found in "dream" lament for Hecuba; at the insistence on physical phenomena as a basis for labeling a stage performance "fiction" and then an apparent disregard for the disjunction in time and place that must mark even stage autobiography; at the hint of a strange blending of offstage and onstage motives when, after saying that the lament for Hecuba is "all for nothing," he apparently envisions "something" in, or as a result of, a stage lament for personal loss; and (since at the moment when one appraises the theatrical effectiveness of one's emotion, that feeling must undergo an alteration) at the implicit claim to the genuine nature of his grief, as opposed to the synthetic nature of grief for Hecuba. It is worth noting that Hamlet's illogical and passionate speech here follows on a passionate declamation on a matter of passion and that his view of the stage here is, characteristically, at odds with much that he later says in his advice to the Player. But perhaps the most important effect of this passage is that we are led to think about differences between various kinds of reality and unreality and to do so by way of references to a dramatic performance.

Other connections between the *Hamlet* characters and stage figures are made in conjunction with an express blending of stage and offstage reality. When Polonius says, "I did enact Julius Caesar: I was killed i' the Capitol; Brutus killed me," Hamlet's answer picks up and emphasizes what he treats as a foolish factual identification of the player with the play role: commenting rather on Polonius than on Caesar, he puns sardonically, "It was a brute part of [Brutus] to kill so capital a calf there" (III.ii.108–11). Yet Hamlet's gibe at Polonius's imprecision follows on a passage where his own insistence on the factual distinction between the Player and Aeneas and the subsequent intimation that there is none between playing oneself and being oneself reveal a questionable estimate of both stage and offstage reality. And when later, in fact, he takes Polonius for a ruler and (in "brute part"?) kills him in the Capitol, the peculiar correspondences between Polonius's play death on some distant inner stage and his "real" death in Denmark provide ironic comment on the words of both Polonius and Hamlet. Hamlet's sword gives the lie to Polonius's earlier claim to having been killed in the Capitol when it gives the claim a dimension of the reality that Hamlet had insisted on. But if the difference between Polonius's play death as Caesar and his real death as Claudius (albeit unintentional the role) illustrates the distinction that Hamlet stresses between "a fiction" and fact, it must also therefore illustrate, for us, the element of reality in what Hamlet calls a "dream," since the death that, comparatively speaking, we label *real* is a matter of seeming. Thus, again, using analogies between Danes and stage figures, Shakespeare manipulates correspondences between dramatic productions to suggest varying distinctions between reality and seeming.

Although the dramatic inset proper appears only in the Player's Speech and the court entertainment, certain stage directions indicate that Shakespeare wants them and a resultant stage business to implement an impression of action-within-action-within-action. We are onlookers as Hamlet and Horatio speak of the impending entertainment; they are onlookers with us as (to the sound of trumpets) the court party enters; we and they are all onlookers as (to the sound of trumpets) the dumb show enters.[5] The flourish to herald the entrance of the King and the Queen of Denmark, just before the same sound for the same purpose marks the appearance of the Player King and the Player Queen, extends the effect of show-within-show. Again, drama is a referent as an implicit analogy between the Danish rulers and imitation rulers invests the former with the unreality of the latter.

Hamlet employs forms of seeming—the "antic disposition," the dumb show, and *Gonzago*—to discover "what our seemers be."[6] He says as much when he tells Horatio that after the play, during which the two of them will watch the show that Claudius presents, they will "both [their] judgements join / In censure of [Claudius's] seeming" (III.ii.91–92). But Shakespeare's use of seeming to unmask seeming ranges far beyond Hamlet's. And when Hamlet says to Horatio as the court party enters, "They are coming to the play; I must be idle" (95), the words hold a significance that Shakespeare does not share with the speaker. For in Hamlet's "idleness" Shakespeare shows us a kind of play-within-play in progress even before the advent of the professional players. And as the association of the King and the Queen of Denmark with an imitation King and Queen who make a similar ceremonious entrance leads us to question the moral substance of the former, so we assess, in the same context, the nature of Hamlet's play-acting. For when Shakespeare informs us, in a scene immediately preceding a dumb show, that consciously or unconsciously the audience is itself already putting on a "show," we find the same convoluted relationships between the real and the representational worlds, the same illumination of the one by the other, that we find in the complex and artful management of the Player's Speech.

When a play contains a dumb show and an interrupted play, a speech taken from a play, criticism of the drama from which the excerpt comes and of drama in general, remarks on a player's performance, a catalogue of drama, reference to roles in amateur theatricals, advice to actors, observations on the nature of drama and the purpose of playing, discussion of the state of the theater in the world of the play and of playwrights and players in that theater, it is not likely that drama, as a subject for consideration, is irrelevant to the playwright's large purpose or to the action of the play. When, in addition, connections are repeatedly drawn between the action of the Danes and "play" action, when events in Elsinore are duplicated in inner-stage drama and former events on an inner stage echoed in Elsinore, then one must suspect that Shakespeare intends the nature of dramatic art to be an index to action in Denmark—perhaps also vice versa. And when a comment served by such connections is iterated in a figurative design wherein the components of a dumb show are informing ingredients and "dumb show" an extended metaphor, then one must conclude that the nature and the intent of drama is the axis on which the meaning of the play turns.

Maynard Mack says that " 'show' seems to be [the] unifying image in 'Hamlet' " and that "the most pervasive of Shakespeare's image patterns . . . is the pattern evolved around the three words, show, act, play."[7] In preceding chapters of this study, we have seen that different denotations in one word may fit it for use in various image patterns: *blast*, for example, appears in an imagery drawn from disease, wind and cold, noise, and mining. Similarly, we have seen that *show* is a word charged with a number of meanings at once and that the "show" imagery is informed by subjects other than dramatic art. If "show" is the unifying image in *Hamlet*, so is "counterfeit presentment," a phrase used to describe a portrait (III.iv.54). And such words as *picture, portrait, painting*, and their derivatives are—like words peculiar to the stage—used in references to hypocrisy, madness, heartlessness, tyranny, vengefulness, unnaturalness, and in accounts of false and inconstant men who prize the imitation.[8] Hamlet uses "the counterfeit presentment of two brothers" to distinguish between the genuine and the fraudulent. If his insistence elsewhere on the insubstantiality of appearance (and on the bad judgment of some picture-prizers) invests this act with an irony he does not intend, his reliance on a portrait is doubly ironic in view of Shakespeare's frequent figurative use of the graphic arts to characterize false-seeming. The phrase "counterfeit presentment" illustrates the way in which different figurative patterns blend: it is a peculiarly apt label for the dumb show; in a less particular sense, it is descriptive of any dramatic production.[9] Moreover, Claudius's "forged process" of King Hamlet's death could aptly be termed a "counterfeit presentment," as could the "forgeries" in speech that Polonius recommends (II.i.20); the praise of Lamond called, in unintentional double entendre, a "forgery" (IV.vii. 90); and the forged letter, on the "fair" writing of which Hamlet commends himself (V.ii.32–36). Thus, the phrase demonstrates, in little, Shakespeare's ability to charge one figurative pattern with the meaning of another. When a pantomime is a "counterfeit presentment" of a murder, then a censure of forged processes may be pertinent to dramatic productions; when "most painted word" and "forged process" say the same thing of Claudius's speech, then a censure of false-seeming in images drawn from painting and portrait may apply to forgeries in speech or action; and when a description of a process of murder suggests both mute tableau and picture, as Pyrrhus stands in momentarily aborted action like a "painted tyrant," then comment in a "world of figures" drawn from dramatic art may interchange with that in an imagery drawn from the graphic arts. Nevertheless, though the figurative definition of "show" is implemented by various referents, "the most pervasive of Shakespeare's image patterns" *is* the one turning on allusions to drama. And it is in the show and the play symbolism, which contains the key to distinctions between seeming and being, that we find the most fascinating and significant comment in the play.

II

Very early in the play Hamlet distinguishes between *being* and *seeming*, and he does so in a language of theater. "Seems, madam!" he exclaims to the Queen when she asks why his father's death "seems . . . so particular with [him],"

> nay, it is; I know not "seems."
> 'Tis not alone my inky cloak, good mother,

. . . .
Nor the dejected 'haviour of the visage,
Together with all forms, moods, shapes of grief,
That can denote me truly: these indeed seem,
For they are actions that a man might play:
But I have that within which passeth show.
                    (I.ii.75–85)

Thus, Hamlet identifies appearance and action on the universal stage with that on the theatrical stage, and uses the word "show" to describe both. By his emphasis on "is," his declaration "I know not 'seems,' " and his reference to "that within" which passes show, he equates *being* with truth and reality, *seeming* with unreality, with something that "a man might play." But, on the other hand, the qualification "alone" implies that "show" can reflect reality: if clothes, tears, forms, moods, and shapes of grief cannot "alone" denote one truly, still the implication is that truth can be thus denoted. And Hamlet is later to give instruction on the kind of playing that "hold[s] . . . the mirror up to nature," a criticism that posits that *seeming* "can denote [man] truly." These two views, not necessarily incompatible, are early clues to what Shakespeare is going to say about proper action on the world stage and to the means he is going to use to say it. For the present, our concern is with the first view: when Hamlet identifies *being* with truth, he gives it a spiritual, rather than a physical, dimension: men may put on the outward signs of grief, but such an action does not add up to "It is."

However, later, in the soliloquy beginning with the words, "To be, or not to be: that is the question" (III.i.56), he departs from his earlier denial that *being* or reality can be circumscribed by the physical and visible. His narrowing of the question he poses is reflected in his limited view of possible courses of acton: a man "in the mind [can] suffer / The slings and arrows of outrageous fortune" or he can "take arms against a sea of troubles." And he implies that "bear[ing] . . . ills," one may live; opposing them, one may end them —that is, die.[10] Thus, his conception here of the alternative choices—to be, or not to be—is defined by actions that *he* sees as alternatives and that *he* posits as options for life or death in the physical sense. His subsequent musings on "non-being," the death that may follow on taking arms (whether against someone else or oneself), are ironic in the light of his own earlier insistence on a "non-being" that may mark the material and external. The man who earlier, declaring his "particularity," says, "I know not 'seems,' " now defines "non-being" in a sense that would allow any man who *breathes* to say, "I know not 'seems.' " And the figurative pattern that links both taking arms and suffering silently to the action of "dumb show" compounds the intimation that Hamlet is now confusing *seeming* with *being*. For Shakespeare makes it quite clear that the two actions Hamlet contemplates are not the only choices, that they are not the proper ones, and that—in an ultimate sense—they are not even alternatives.

Let us review these three points. First, that they are not the only possible choices is obvious in a play where even Claudius's appeal to Norway results in good. Claudius chooses neither "to take arms" nor "in the mind to suffer . . . fortune" in the person of Fortinbras. Instead, he resorts to reason and an appeal to proper rule, and war is averted. One may say that Claudius's problem of a threatened evil and Hamlet's problem of an entrenched evil are so different that choice, in the two circumstances, is not comparable. But the King's response to the aggressiveness of Fortinbras is just one detail in Shakespeare's persistent questioning of the wisdom in either a resort to violence or a passive acceptance of misfortune. We have seen that both event and image suggest that "tak[ing] arms" is a dubious choice: King Hamlet's decision to fight with King Fortinbras is still causing trouble thirty years later; the First Clown's pun about Adam as "the first that ever bore arms" in a context of his being the first "grave-maker" (V.i.35–38) and in a play that repeatedly reminds us of the effect of Adam's sin, calls in question the bearing of arms; the very phrase, "to take arms against a *sea* of troubles," brilliantly connects the decision for violence with "go[ing] to [the] water," in *Hamlet* wrong choice, whether willing or unwilling; and the use of weapons of war is insistently linked with noise and show.

As for the advisability of "suffer[ing] / The slings and arrows of outrageous fortune," Shakespeare certainly questions the nature of, and profit in, this choice—at least, as Hamlet understands it. If Horatio represents Hamlet's view of stoic and patient fortitude—and Hamlet praises him as "one, in suffering all, that suffers nothing" (III.ii.71)—then Shakespeare furnishes no defense for this alternative to bearing arms. Three times Horatio tries to influence Hamlet, each time *not* to act: not to follow the Ghost (after Marcellus initiates the warning); not to rant over Ophelia's grave; and not to duel with Laertes. But he never suggests a positive course of action for Hamlet to follow. And even in his negative advice, particularly in the last two instances, he proves rather unresisting than not. An acquiescence to Hamlet's words and deeds generally marks Horatio; in his exchanges with Hamlet, he is increasingly given to taciturn and ambiguous agreement and exclamation, a development that puts Hamlet's comment on him into ironic perspective. If Horatio is one who "suffer[s] all," the prime example we are given of such a practice on his part is his suffering of Hamlet's decisions and actions. And if this adds up to Horatio's "suffer[ing] nothing," it certainly brings no good to anybody else.

Even Polonius takes it for granted that giving one's "heart a winking, mute and dumb," that "play[ing] the desk or table-book," is irresponsible (II.ii.136–37), though when Polonius goes "round to work," he takes the wrong action. But just as Horatio passively attends Hamlet, he remains in court, Hamlet gone, in passive attendance on Claudius; and although Shakespeare could have easily justified that stay and attendance with a request from Hamlet, instead he uses it to accentuate the nature of Horatio's acceptance of "fortune" and to make the point that even when Horatio counsels action, his advice is inadequate, no more affirmative than his advice to Hamlet *not* to act. Of the "distract" Ophelia, Horatio advises Gertrude, " 'Twere good she were spoken with: for she may strew / Dangerous conjectures in ill-breeding minds" (IV.v.14–15). Even if one considers it not impracticable to try to talk a mad girl into being reasonable, such advice strikes a note of too little, too late. One wonders at Horatio's belated and enigmatic concern, if not for a King whose right to rule he has reason to doubt, for a general welfare he has not evoked on more timely occasions. His ineffectualness is further implied by the intimation that he is the one appointed to "follow [Ophelia] close" and "give her good watch" (75). If he is, as Hamlet says, not a man whom fortune can affect (and this, like all of Hamlet's other assessments of character, proves questionable), neither is he a man who makes a forceful and appropriate effort to affect fortune. And at the end of the play, either the error in Hamlet's judgment of him as one who "in suffering all . . . suffers nothing" or the inadequacy of Horatio's philosophy when put to the test is revealed: this man, described as one who takes "fortune's buffets" with "thanks" (III.ii.72–73), decides to take them with poison. Thus, his conception of the options open to man and of the nature of those options proves not unlike that expressed by Hamlet, for Horatio's alternative to suffering "in the mind" is "to take arms against a sea of troubles" and to become one of a group of people who are all, in a sense, suicides.

None of this is to deny Horatio high-mindedness, nobility of utterance, and regard for Hamlet. Nevertheless, however removed from purposed wrong, he is never shown as a constructive force for good. Although his good intentions are not to be doubted on the only three occasions when he counsels action, the peculiar similarities and differences in these three pieces of advice reveal the Horatio-of-inaction in the Horatio-of-action. Like his counsel that the mad Ophelia be "spoken with," his other two recommendations involve speaking to someone: at the beginning of the play, the "dreaded sight" of "fear and wonder" (which he describes as "prologue to the omen coming on") leads to his "advice" to Marcellus that they let Hamlet know what they have seen; at the end of the play, the "dismal sight" of "woe or wonder" (which he would remove to a "stage" while he provides an epilogue) leads to his advice to Fortinbras that he, Horatio, tell the "yet unknowing world / How these things came about" (I.i.25,44,123, 168–70;V.ii.378,374,389–91). The reason he gives to Fortinbras (to avoid "more mischance" from "wild minds") recalls a latent irony in the reason he gives to Marcellus ("As needful in our loves, fitting our duty") and in the reason he gives to Gertrude for speaking with the deranged Ophelia (to avoid danger from "ill-breeding minds"). One does not question Horatio's honesty when, at the end of the play, he expresses to Fortinbras, as earlier to Gertrude, a concern for the general welfare. Nevertheless, such a reason for addressing the "world" does follow incongruously on his own aborted suicide and does depart from the motive for storytelling that Hamlet has given him. Perhaps both of these points are to his credit. But (despite any case one may make in his favor, despite the plausibility of his express reason and the fact that "more mischance" is always possible) his belated solicitude for avoiding "plots and errors" (V.ii.406) and the ineptitude of the phrase "*more* mischance" reinforces the general impression of Horatio's detachment from reality and the consequent inadequacy of his attempts to cope with it, however well-meaning his intentions or civic-minded his advice. Perhaps Shakespeare shows us, by way of Horatio, the effect of habitual aloofness or patient submission on the ability to act meaningfully and constructively. However that may be, there is reason to conclude that insofar as Horatio exemplifies Hamlet's conception of the suffering of fortune, one alternative contemplated in the "to be, or not to be" soliloquy is defined by Horatio's futile, tardy, or inconsequential responses to circumstance.

The figurative relationships between "tak[ing] arms" and "noise" and between a mute suffering and "dumbness" are obvious. Thus, my third point—that in an ultimate sense the two courses of action are not alternatives—is a burden of the pattern we have traced. Hamlet names a choice of noise or a choice of dumbness as his two options, but Shakespeare, who makes the two interchangeable, defines both as a choice for seeming and "dumb show."

Nevertheless, Hamlet is expressing in this soliloquy a thesis of Shakespeare's figurative comment: "To be, or not to be" *is* the question. But the choice of *being* presupposes a comprehension of the nature of reality. If we can say that early in the play Hamlet makes a distinction between *being* and *seeming* that is in accord with Shakespeare's show symbolism and that later when he defines *being* as physical existence and a dumb suffering as a means to such *being*, he departs from his own earlier definition, still the matter is complicated by the fact that in his earlier speech he also implies that *seeming* may contain truth. And if a form of theater becomes Shakespeare's symbol for unreality, the very fact that the argument is presented in dramatic form argues that another form of theater may be a symbol for reality. Let us turn to Hamlet's dramatic criticism, for in his observations about reality and unreality in the theater lies a key to Shakespeare's essential comment on proper choice, proper action, and the nature of *being*.

Hamlet censures actors who "split . . . ears," "tear a passion to tatters," o'er-do Termagant, out-herod Herod, strut and bellow (III.ii.10,11,15,37). Such criticism is directed against lack of judgment, reason, and rule, a failure that (as the phrases above demonstrate) he connects with noise. The fault he most deplores is an excess that destroys the illusion of reality, for even on the stage fundamental and universal rule must operate: anything "overdone" is "from the purpose of playing" (22) and the actor who would "hold . . . the mirror up to nature" (24) is bound by nature's rules. The various examples he gives of intemperance on the stage, of departure from rule and therefore from reality, are not mutually exclusive; but we may say that besides criticizing the actor who does not observe the *limits* of his role, he names the actor who "come[s] tardy off" (27) or misrepresents the *nature* of the role: who does not "suit the action to the word, the word to the action" (19–20); who, playing Christian, pagan, or man, does not employ "the accent of Christians nor the gait of Christian, pagan, nor man" (35–36); who, though it is his job to hold "the mirror up to nature," "imitate[s] humanity . . . abominably" (39–40). And he finds fault with the actor who is not faithful to the *purpose* of the role, the playwright, or playing: who "speak[s] . . . more than is set down for [him]," laughs, and adds a superfluous clowning (44–46), all of which (though it may set "barren spectators" to laughing) is "villanous," Hamlet says, "and shows a most

pitiful ambition in the fool that uses it" (49–50); for besides
obscuring the intentions of the playwright, the Clown who
indulges in, or invites, an irrelevant laughter defeats his own
purposes. In effect, Hamlet says that a player who lacks control, art, or understanding is unable to image actuality; if he
exhibits a self-interest, he cannot properly serve the ends of
playing.

Hamlet's dramatic criticism is interesting in itself. But,
more importantly, it provides Shakespeare with a means to
a great variety of indirect comment. First, such criteria are
obviously applicable to the dramatic performances within the
play: one is led to wonder whether the First Player's Speech
(which is followed by Hamlet's most passionate soliloquy)
"beget[s] a temperance"; whether the court performance, in
its repetitiveness, is "overdone" and thus "from the purpose
of playing." Second, since almost all of the principals of
Hamlet at some time dissemble in a kind of play-action and
are repeatedly identified with actors, since Hamlet himself
puts on an "antic disposition," one is led to look at their conduct in the light of Hamlet's advice. Third, one is struck by
the ironic appositeness between the dramatic action that
Hamlet says can*not* reflect mankind and the action that he,
as a man, adopts.

This is not to say that his dramatic criticism is contradicted by Shakespeare's dramatic practice. At the risk of belaboring the obvious, let me reiterate a point touched on
above. When Hamlet censures, for example, "bellowing," he
is decrying excess in the player. He does not deny that men in
real life may bellow or that an actor may have to play a bel-
lower; he does not say that Herods and Termagants should not
be presented on the stage: he simply does not address himself to such particulars, although he does explicitly allow for
a dramatic projection of excess, "a whirlwind of . . . passion" (III.ii.7).[11] His sights are aimed at the player's artistry,
rather than any specific subject matter. And without falsify-
ing what he *says*, one could add that if a player plays a
Herod-like character, he must not "out-herod Herod"; if the
role calls for "out-herod[ing] Herod," such action is in order.
Certainly, to argue that the illusion of reality is destroyed

when a player "overdoes" is not to argue that "overdoing" cannot be realistically dramatized. Nor is there any essential contradiction in his declaring of the world of Denmark that "things rank and gross in nature / Possess it merely" (I.ii. 136–37) and then insisting that a true dramatic mirroring of the world depends on an observance of the "modesty of nature." For it does not follow that the artist who depicts an unruly man can ignore rule. The fact that Hamlet splits ears and tears a passion to tatters, that he fails to suit action to word, points to *his* departure (not Shakespeare's) from a universal and natural rule that, according to his argument, is the touchstone to offstage, as well as onstage, action. The very medium in which Hamlet's criticism appears must attest to its validity: if, for example, the actor portraying Hamlet betrays a self-preoccupation, he does not project the reality of the character, however self-preoccupied the latter is.

However, undertones in Hamlet's dramatic criticism suggest that his dramatic application of the rule he espouses would differ from Shakespeare's. Conceding that he explicitly allows for a "torrent, tempest, and . . . whirlwind of . . . passion" on the stage and that an admonition against a method that oversteps does not exclude the representation of a man who oversteps or reject anything in nature as a matter for dramatic portrayal, still one can hardly ignore the difference in his emphasis when he contemplates "nature" in his world of Denmark and when, to the players, he evokes the rules of "nature" that implement a stage reflection of that world. Although he frequently describes men as beasts and although the actor would therefore have to imitate the beast in holding the mirror up to such a man, Hamlet criticizes players who imitate humanity abominably as if they had only men, not beasts, to imitate. He may be talking about technique in acting; but he does so by way of an assumption that denies the validity of the thing portrayed. Yet, by evidence of his own comment elsewhere, there are men whom one might think made by "nature's journeymen" (III.ii.38). One wonders whether he wants a particular nature reflected on the stage, whatever his general claims. And when he so sweepingly scorns "inexplicable dumb-shows and noise," one wonders whether he is attacking the wrong use of form and means or whether he implies that a certain device per se and noisy men and events serve no useful purposes in a dramatic imaging of existence.

If we look back to his remarks on the Player's Speech, we find the same ambiguities, the same possibility that he would censor certain aspects of nature on the stage. He calls the play from which the Player's Speech is taken "an excellent play . . . set down with as much modesty as cunning" and says that it has been praised for having "no matter in the phrase that might indict the author of affectation" and "no sallets in the lines to make the matter savoury" (II.ii.459–64). Here again the quality of "modesty" is his touchstone; but again it is debatable just what he thinks the playwright's exercise of "modesty" involves. One can argue that he is emphasizing the need for judgment, taste, and discrimination in the handling of any subject matter, not excluding any matter in itself. But always while he professes to be commenting on "honest method" in writing and acting, there is a hint in his criticism that certain aspects of nature are not amenable to "method," that they are somehow so inherently "immodest" or "affected" that they are not subject to rule or art. One may find in this a reasonable warning (perhaps even a pertinent one for our own time); but the question is the extent to which Hamlet carries it. The language in the Player's Speech, which he admires, is rather extravagant than not; but we note that though the matter concerns a "hellish" man, that man is presented in description and declamation, rather than in action. So long as Hamlet is espousing a technique that has recourse to universal rule, one can believe that he expresses Shakespeare's own convictions. But if he implies that certain ugly aspects of actuality would be better excluded from the stage (or consigned to narration and rhetoric), if he implies that matter itself is "affected" or that beastly men should not be *enacted* or that "noise" and "sallets" cannot serve any proper dramatic purpose, then he has less faith in the art of the playwright and actor than Shakespeare has, and a more limited view of theater.

But though Hamlet disdains "dumb-shows and noise" as

if the stage should eliminate or soft-pedal a certain matter, as well as a certain means, he characteristically employs them. We see again his habitual inconsistency in his sponsorship of a device he belittles and of a drama essentially at odds with the spirit of the precepts he urges on the players. Even more significant than the comment afforded on Hamlet's character is the demonstration of the nature and purpose of two kinds of theater, the difference between his dramatic practice and Shakespeare's, though both employ dumb shows. Hamlet, bent on mirroring a woman's inconstancy and a man's treachery to an admirable ruler and kinsman, does not desire the players to "beget a temperance"; nor does he suit his own action to his words to the players, for he chooses and provides words for a play that must be artificial, whatever methods the actors use: Gonzago is all-moralizer, all-wise, all-erred against; Baptista is all excessive protest of fidelity; Lucianus all-villain; and the action itself is presented in extravagant repetition. The nature of the court entertainment does not so much contradict as support the intimations that what Hamlet really wants on the stage is an idealized version of nature; for although his purpose leads him to choose a play that reflects a wicked deed, a villain in action, the conception in it of good and evil is unrealistic and arbitrary. Such a play no more holds the mirror up to nature than it aims at the other general purposes of theater articulated by Hamlet. And quite aside from the particular private aims for it that Hamlet has declared (to "catch the conscience of the king" or to unkennel occulted guilt), his observations to the other onlookers reveal that he employs theater to project and implement his malice, scorn, and grief; to whet his anger; to effect the antithesis of the ends of drama as he has defined those ends. Obviously, his purpose in commissioning this performance is not the one he has laid down for the players; and he is willing to utilize a dumb show, not because he sees it as a dramatic method for reflecting reality, but because (like the "extravagant and erring spirit" that sets him on his course) he has it in him to be extravagant, to overdo, to err against his better judgment and knowledge.

But Shakespeare, in employing a dumb show, excess, and

extravagance, holds to the proposition that the theatrical stage must reflect the universal one. And seeing the world of human nature as a "mingled web" of good and evil, Shakespeare does not draw easy distinctions between the two by way of bloodless "puppets." The contrast between *Gonzago* and *Hamlet* contains implicit comment on the proper nature of dramatic art; similarly, the proper purpose of drama may be glimpsed in the difference between Hamlet's use of, and reaction to, the characters in the play-within-the-play and Shakespeare's manipulation of our response to Hamlet. The latter, who habitually enunciates admirable principles he himself does not observe, purposes to hold the inconsistency of the Player Queen up to censure and Baptista's words to scorn because of her deed; himself erring, he sits in uncharitable judgment on erring humanity, rejecting the man with the fault in his dramatic projection of actuality as in life; and he espouses, by way of theater, the most unqualified and unbending view of the nature and the act of the sinner. But Shakespeare gives Hamlet his due for what he nobly says, despite what he ignobly does; evokes our recognition of his good while detailing his evil; and "beget[s] a temperance" in the reader toward an intemperate man. From what we see of "The Mouse-trap," we can infer that, at most, it aims at some such static moral instruction as "Crime does not pay." From what we see of Hamlet's use of it, we know that though in holding up to the wrongdoer his "own image" he may say that he intends to catch the sinner's conscience, he proposes in that event no constructive consequence. But Shakespeare does not sit in self-appointed judgment on human beings; nor is he given to the moral stance enclosed in "thou shalt nots."

But while neither Hamlet's contempt for, nor his use of, dumb shows and noise as dramatic matter and means may be said to mark the limits of Shakespeare's literal viewpoint and practice, what Hamlet would exclude from the theatrical stage becomes the symbol for the unreality (the "dumb-shows and noise") that Shakespeare would exclude from the universal stage; what Hamlet finds "from the purpose of playing" becomes Shakespeare's criteria for what is *from the purpose of being;* and in Hamlet's description of a stage action

131

that "hold[s] . . . the mirror up to nature," Shakespeare
points to the kind of action that makes for reality, rather
than unreality, on the world stage. By way of Hamlet's dramatic criticism Shakespeare details and reinforces the sometimes more general definitions of proper conduct and choice
that we have noted in other passages in the play. Thus, if a
man is to "pass show," if he is to say, "I know not 'seems,'"
he must "acquire and beget a temperance." So observing "the
modesty of nature," he reflects fair judgment, God-like reason, and proper rule; he takes his fellowmen in, using them
according to his "own honour and dignity," rather than their
desert; he feeds Christ and has God at his table. And so doing, he chooses the reality that passes show, and makes the
decision "to be." The decision "not to be" is the choice of
dumbness and noise. Marked by passion, madness, and disorder, the essential character of false-seeming is found in
Hamlet's description of unnatural stage action. The man who
splits ears and out-herods Herod; who fails to suit deed to
noble word; who, putting on the semblance of a beast, imitates humanity abominably; whose self-absorption reflects
a "pitiful ambition" and leads him to forget the purpose of
being and the aims of his creator—such a man makes the
decision for "show."

Thus, Shakespeare uses Hamlet's distinctions between
proper and improper "action" on the smaller stage to distinguish between proper and improper action on the larger one
and to define ultimate reality and unreality. Such an analogy
has the effect of investing the material world with the character of an illusory one: on both stages the player is faced
with the choice of *being* or *seeming*, though *seeming* is the
medium through which *being* is revealed, perpetuated, initiated. Although the analogy is primarily a means to comment
on human conduct, it works in two ways, extending the dramatic criticism itself. That is, the "reality" on the smaller
stage, in mirroring an illusory world, must reflect both good
and evil; but good theater on it, as on the larger stage, is
determined by the degree to which the player images what
Shakespeare elsewhere calls "great creating nature."[12] However, the primary burden of the figurative comparison is that

"to be, or not to be" *is* the question facing a man at every turn of his performance on the world stage. And as Shakespeare is employing a not uncommon analogy, he is presenting, by means of it, a not uncommon view of the nature of man's essential choice: Donne, for example, expresses exactly the same uncompromising doctrine when he says, "Man lives under another manner of law [than the 'creatures'] . . . doe this, and you shall live; disobey, and you shall die. But yet, the choise is yours: Choose ye this day life, or death."[13] Any doubt that Shakespeare is giving to a familiar analogy unfamiliar form and to a common doctrine on the character of man's basic options uncommon development in a rich and sustained figurative comment on the difference between *being* and *seeming* may be dispelled by a study of the scene in Gertrude's closet, where the action is explicitly described in theatrical terms; the nature and the effect of both "show" and the action that "passeth show" are demonstrated; and the thesis that *seeming* is a medium for change (good or bad) is explicitly declared.

III

Hamlet says to his mother, "I set you up a glass / Where you may see the inmost part of you" (III.iv.19–20); but unlike the player or the playwright who would hold the mirror up to nature, he is bent on reflecting only the evil in her. His words are described as "noise": "What have I done," she asks, "that thou darest wag thy tongue / In noise so rude against me?" (39–40). They are described as weapons: "These words, like daggers, enter in mine ears" (95). His anger and violence arouse in Gertrude a wrathful movement toward reprisal: "Nay, then, I'll set those to you that *can speak*" (17, italics mine). His noise and disorder generate confusion: "What act, / That roars so loud, and thunders in the index?" (51–52). His passion elicits despair: what he shows her in her soul is, she says, "such black and grained spots / As *will not leave their tinct*" (89–91, italics mine). He resorts to an extravagant use of abusive epithets: Claudius is "a mildew'd ear," a "moor," "a murderer and a villain," "a slave," "a vice of kings," "a cut-purse," "a king of shreds and patches" (64, 67,96–102); and his excess evokes in *her* a futile repetition: "no more . . . no more . . . No more . . . No more!" (88, 94,96,101). If he proposes to "set [her] up a glass," neither method nor effect suggests the nature and purpose of good theater. On the contrary, an assault on "ears" recalls a method of destruction; and the whole passage is obliquely reminiscent of "dumb-shows and noise."

But when, instead of ranting and bellowing, Hamlet acquires a temperance, he begets one; when, not treating her according to what he thinks are her deserts, he suggests a positive course of action—"Confess yourself to heaven; / Repent what's past; avoid what is to come" (149–50)—he sparks a response quite different from her earlier hopelessness: "What shall I do?" (180). Hamlet has just foisted the death of Polonius first on "fortune" (32) and then on "heaven" (173), and this transference of responsibility for his own act is to burgeon into a glorification of the means by which he "seal'd" the plot against Rosencrantz and Guildenstern: "Even in that was heaven ordinant" (V.ii.48). But such insistence on Hamlet's increasing subjection to violence and self-delusion highlights Shakespeare's demonstration of the power for good in the corrupted understanding and the positive response that power can set in motion. After an exchange where dumbness and noise produce only dumbness and noise, the revelation that even a limited exercise of reason and temperance also operates in chain reaction accentuates the relative futility of the first action and the constructiveness of the second.

Whether Hamlet properly directs Gertrude's willingness to submit herself to a rule that says, "Confess yourself to heaven; repent" is another matter. We may note, however, that he makes two requests to her, both negative. The first—that she "go not to [the King's] bed" (III.iv.159)—she does not answer. But this request is accompanied by an enjoinder to a positive course of action; and if the "black and grained spots" that she laments are the lust that Hamlet accuses her of, then there is, later in the play, a hint that she does try to change "their tinct" by "assum[ing] a virtue," as well as practicing an abstinence that Hamlet urges on her: Claudius is subsequently to say, "I see, *in passages of proof*, / Time qualifies the spark and fire of [love]" (IV.vii.113–14, italics mine). The other request—that she not reveal "this matter" to the King—she answers, "If words be made of breath, / And breath of life, I have no life to breathe / What thou hast said to me" (III.iv.197–99); and we know that she not only keeps this promise but elaborates on it in a blameworthy fashion. But whether Hamlet uses for good or evil the ascendancy that he gets over his mother, Shakespeare shows us that when he refrains from noisy recrimination and exerts some forbearance, a restraint that extends beyond a mere determination *not* to do what Nero did (III.ii.411–12), Gertrude reacts without her earlier anger, confusion, dumbness, despair, and vain repetition. The process seen in action is also glimpsed in his declaration, "And when you are desirous to be bless'd, / I'll blessing beg of you" (III.iv.171–72). But though these words reinforce the dramatic revelation that a motion toward goodness is creative of other movements toward good and though they reflect Hamlet's willingness to return good for good, they also point to a limitation in him: the difficult action—to initiate the good, to respond nobly to what he sees as evil—he never greatly achieves. However, in this scene, after first indulging in vain vituperation, he does attain some judgment, reason, and rule—enough that we are shown, in one passage, the relative effect of unreal and real action.

In this same scene, there is also a direct statement that *seeming* may implement reality or unreality, good or evil. Hamlet expresses a philosophy of "action":

> Assume a virtue, if you have it not.
> That monster, custom, who all sense doth eat,
> Of habits devil, is angel yet in this,
> That to the use of actions fair and good
> He likewise gives a frock or livery,
> That aptly is put on. Refrain to-night,
> And that shall lend a kind of easiness
> To the next abstinence: the next more easy;
> For use almost can change the stamp of nature,

And either . . . the devil, or throw him out
With wondrous potency.

(III.iv.160–70)[14]

In urging Gertrude to "put on" the appearance of a virtue, Hamlet is not advocating hypocrisy, the "most painted word," the *show* that hides the ugly intention or fact, but the assumption of an appearance of good with the intention of making *seeming* a reality. He stresses two ideas: the need to affect actions "fair and good" and the power of "habit" or "use." The great significance in a declaration that an external practice contains the seed for internal change lies less in its bearing on what Gertrude may do than on what Hamlet does. If a habitual assumption of a virtue can almost change the essential character of the seemer, then one is led to wonder about the effect of a habitual pretense to madness.

That habit or custom may be destructive is not a late assertion in *Hamlet*. In the first act, when Hamlet calls the King's rouse "a custom / More honour'd in the breach than the observance," he goes on to declare that "the o'er-growth of some complexion" may break down "the pales and forts of reason" and to name, as one of the causes for the corruption of the noble substance, "some habit that too much o'er-leavens / The form of plausive manners," an idea he now repeats when he tells Gertrude that "use almost can change the stamp of nature." His language to his mother—"to the use of actions fair and good / [Custom] gives a frock or livery, / That aptly is put on"—echoes his description of his own action when he earlier determines "to put an antic disposition on" (I.v.172). And by way of Hamlet's repeated and strong insistence on the power of habit (a theme to be reiterated in a speech by Horatio in Act V), Shakespeare throws a sharp light on Hamlet's pretense to madness and illuminates his conduct and his open declaration of madness in the final act.

Near the end of the play, after saying that he has "done [Laertes] wrong" and asking pardon, Hamlet first ascribes the killing of Polonius to his madness; then, not content with this, he resorts to an exercise of logic to show that *he* did not wrong Laertes:

> What I have done,
> That might your nature, honour and exception
> Roughly awake, I here proclaim was madness.
> Was't Hamlet wrong'd Laertes? Never Hamlet:
> If Hamlet from himself be ta'en away,
> And when he's not himself does wrong Laertes,
> Then Hamlet does it not, Hamlet denies it.
> Who does it, then? His madness: if 't be so,
> Hamlet is of the faction that is wrong'd;
> His madness is poor Hamlet's enemy.
> (V.ii.241–50)

Since, on other occasions, he supplements the "act" of madness with the word, claiming that his "wit's diseased" (III. ii.333–34), it may be argued that he is here only doing what he has done before; that he is hiding behind a mask to conceal his purpose and excuse his actions; that, moreover, deception here is thrust on him, since he dare not say he killed Polonius thinking him Claudius. Yet there is a difference between this elaboration on the lie and the laconic "My wit's diseased," a difference hardly explainable by mere circumstance. After the altercation with Laertes in the graveyard and not long before he speaks these words, he says to Horatio, "I am very sorry . . . That to Laertes I forgot myself . . . I'll court his favours" (V.ii.75–78). Now by way of showing that he is sorry he "forgot [him]self," he uses his own name seven times in seven lines and refers to himself fourteen times in ten lines. By way of courting the favors of a man who has a sister and "a noble father lost" (IV.vii.25), he says, "But pardon 't, as you are a gentleman" (V.ii.238) and, after characteristically turning the tables and putting the injured man on trial (and with an offhand phrase that might appear to Laertes to slight the importance of the matter), he goes on to angle for sympathy for "poor Hamlet." By way of reinforcing an excuse of madness, he employs a show of considerable mental agility. Certainly, he is not intentionally demonstrating the "sore distraction" he tells Laertes he is "punish'd" with (240-41). But there is, paradoxically, in this exercise of logic an element of unreason and unreality that exceeds conscious equivocation.

What strikes one particularly is not just the inconsistency or irony in his intimating that "pardon" is the recourse of the "gentleman"; in his expecting Laertes to react to injury with a nobility that he, Hamlet, the self-appointed instructor of all around him, has not shown; in his arguing for a distinction between the trespass and the trespasser when the latter is himself. We have seen many instances of his inconsistency, and we have heard him use "reason [to] pandar will." It is not just the ironic perspective his earlier rebuke to Gertrude throws on his own words here: he has said,

> Mother, for love of grace,
> Lay not that flattering unction to your soul,
> That not your trespass, but my madness speaks:
> It will but skin and film the ulcerous place,
> Whiles rank corruption, mining all within,
> Infects unseen.
>
> (III.iv.144–49)

Now he moves beyond mere qualification of trespass to the "flattering unction" he has warned Gertrude against, and denies the trespass in arguing that it was his madness that "spoke" with daggers. Nor is it just the parallel with Claudius that strikes us here: that the man whose favors could not be courted by Claudius proposes to "court [the] favours" of the son of *his* victim; that *he* now thinks, as Claudius has done, to explain murder away with a "forged process," and thus subscribes to a course of action that he, of all people, should consider unprofitable. And it is not just the progression in his disregard for proportion and fact, the movement from a sincere advocacy of principles that he, himself, does not abide by, to the deliberate and *superfluous* hypocrisy here in portraying himself as victim to the man whose father he has slain. Hamlet honestly wishes to propitiate Laertes; and what shocks one most about his words is the absurdity of an argument that, intending to gain the regard of a grieving son and brother, focuses on "poor Hamlet," rather than on poor Ophelia or poor Polonius or poor Laertes.

If such an argument could placate Laertes, it would have to come from someone else. Hamlet's recourse to logic must have the effect on Laertes of weakening his claim to madness; his reduction of the murder of Polonius to syllogism, a self-pitying one at that, can hardly conciliate; and a use of premise and deduction to deny that he has wronged Laertes, particularly when the premise is self-commendation and the deduction self-commiseration, is hardly a sensible way of seeking pardon. Earlier, Claudius has implied that if Laertes does not avenge his father, he is "like the painting of a sorrow" (IV.vii. 109); and Hamlet has declared to Horatio that he sees the "portraiture" of Laertes' cause by the "image" of his own (V.ii.77–78). Despite the declared parallel, one suspects that this imagery, so often used to define the counterfeit and the unreal, characterizes Hamlet's view of Laertes' loss in *contrast* to his own: that, to him, Laertes' sorrow *is* insubstantial, a painted replica of the real image. Such a view would, to some degree, qualify the falsehood, inconsistency, hypocrisy, and egocentricity in his speech to Laertes. But one must still be shocked by this illogical use of logic, by the extent of his departure from reason and rule. Yet the revelation is in line with Shakespeare's insistent thematic comment on the power of use and habit, a point reiterated in the last act when—in an instance of the irony in continual play throughout this act —Hamlet's taste is offended by the Clown's singing at grave-digging and Horatio says, "Custom hath made it in him a property of easiness" (V.i.75–76). Such a premise surely illuminates the involuntary "madness" of Hamlet's words to Laertes. Though the Hamlet of the first act saw the matter of his father's death as "particular," he was not then the man who here employs a show of logic to make falsehood pass for truth: deception has become, through custom, a "property of easiness" and the line between "is" and "seems" fluid; the prince who once said, "I know not 'seems,' " now knows almost nothing else; the use of madness has "almost changed the stamp of nature"; and by a habitual use of *show*, he is indeed "mad in craft."

FIGURATIVE DESIGN IN *HAMLET*

It follows that he speaks a truth he does not apprehend when he claims that his madness wronged Laertes and that this madness is his enemy. Earlier, after he leaps into Ophelia's grave and Laertes grapples with him saying, "The devil take thy soul" (281), he directs a lengthy, violent, and contemptuous tirade at Laertes, incongruously concluding it with the question, "What is the reason that you use me thus? / I loved you ever" (312–13). If Hamlet has reason to hate Claudius, who has also declared love for the son of his victim (I.ii.110–12), then Laertes, who has also heard an injunction to "remember" (IV.v.176;cf.I.v.91), has reason to hate Hamlet. But now Hamlet, after killing Laertes' father, wonders what *reason* Laertes has to act as he does. It might be argued that although Hamlet's "towering passion" (V.ii.80) is spontaneous, the question he puts to Laertes and the protestation of love, followed immediately by the ugly lines, "But it is no matter; / Let Hercules himself do what he may, / The cat will mew and dog will have his day," are calculatingly mad. But the question is characteristic of a state of mind consistently revealed in Hamlet's speech in the last act. And it also affords Shakespeare two important observations: first, implicitly, a desire for revenge is not the effect of reason; second, a desire for revenge is not productive of reason. One recalls that Horatio has feared that the Ghost "might deprive [Hamlet's] sovereignty of reason / And draw [him] into madness" (I.iv.73–74). All signs point to the conclusion that it *is* Hamlet's madness that has wronged Laertes, but it is a madness that lies below the mask. And madness *is* Hamlet's enemy: the "antic disposition," the "habit" his desire for revenge takes, has changed his noble substance. His irrational question and irrelevant declaration of love, in the midst of an insulting verbal onslaught, demonstrate his fall from reason.

The challenge Hamlet issues to Laertes over the grave of Ophelia, his offer to duel on the "theme" of love (V.i.289–94), is cut from the same cloth as the challenge he subsequently receives to duel on the theme of honor. The rationale behind his challenge recalls that of the Ghost, who thinks that an act of violence will prove love and grief: "If thou didst ever thy dear father love . . . Revenge his foul and most unnatural murder." It recalls the reasoning of Polonius, who thinks that an "act" of madness proves love and grief: "He, repelled [by Ophelia] . . . Fell . . . Into the madness wherein now he raves" (II.ii.146–50). Now Hamlet proposes that he and Laertes determine the greater lover and griever by acts of violence or madness: by fighting, tearing themselves, drinking vinegar, eating a crocodile (V.i.298–99). To say that Hamlet is merely defining figuratively the lengths to which he will go for love is not to the point: when even fasting and weeping, which one might more naturally connect with grief and love than eating a crocodile, become a basis for competition, love is not the question. Nor can one say that Hamlet is merely thus expressing his contempt for rant. We can concede that he has no way of knowing what we know: that after the deaths of Polonius and Ophelia, Laertes speaks, for the most part, with remarkable brevity and directness; that on his return to Denmark, in his first words to Claudius, he says succinctly what Hamlet, for all his talk, never says, "O thou vile king, / Give me my father!" (IV.v.115–16). Nevertheless, for Hamlet to accuse the man he has injured of whining, prating, mouthing, trying to "outface" *him;* to rant at length over what he calls "the bravery of [that man's] grief" (V.ii.79); and to turn from a distress he has, in large part, brought about, with a contemptuous reference to cat and dog—all this is of a piece with his later callous dismissal of the deaths of Rosencrantz and Guildenstern and his subsequent resort to self-extenuating argument on the matter of Polonius's death. Injustice and irrationality are, Shakespeare implies, inevitable by-products of isolation, of a loss of contact with ultimate reality. Though Hamlet later says he "forgot [him] self," the one thing he is evidently incapable of forgetting is himself: only his wrongs have weight; only his griefs are important. Imprisoned in self, he lies "worse than the mutines in the bilboes."

Thus, Shakespeare provides graphic comment on the pitfalls in Polonius's unqualified advice, "To thine own self be true."[15] As Hamlet switches and equivocates, giving first one and then another interpretation of his killings, one sees the impossibility of his being true "to any man" (or, in the long run, to himself) when self marks the boundaries of his world. To Gertrude and Horatio, he ascribes his murders to Heaven, to fortune, or to the will of his victims; to Laertes and the court, he blames his madness and fortune. And whoever or whatever he credits for the murders, for whatever reason, he evades responsibility. Polonius is an "intruding fool" (III. iv.31); similarly, the "defeat" of Rosencrantz and Guildenstern is the result of their "insinuation" (V.ii.59). Though he has casually killed a father and has treacherously sent men to death without "shriving-time allow'd" ("O, horrible! O, horrible! most horrible!" says the Ghost of this same action), he exhibits no sense of guilt, no awareness of the "heavy burthen" that even Claudius laments (III.i.54). He may declare to Gertrude that he "repents" the death of Polonius, but he immediately refers the killing to the pleasure of Heaven (why it should "please" Heaven to "scourge" the court of Polonius, rather than Claudius, he does not say; except when it is convenient to explicate Heaven's movings, Hamlet allows Heaven to move in mysterious ways); and nothing in his immediate reaction or his later conduct to Laertes implies repentance or remorse. He may say that he "wrong'd" Laertes, but he immediately contradicts the saying—and on the basis of a lie. What is implicit in all this is explicit in his words on the deaths of Rosencrantz and Guildenstern: "They are not near my conscience" (V.ii.58). All of his equivocations have an element of truth in them: fortune, Heaven, and his madness do play a role in the murders; what the victims themselves do is certainly a factor in their physical undoing. But one cannot assign Polonius's death to chance when the hand that strikes the blow intends murder; and one cannot say that Rosencrantz and Guildenstern come between "the fell incensed points / Of mighty opposites" (61–62) when Hamlet's point is directed at them. Moreover, it is one thing to say that Heaven is ordinant in all of these deaths in the play and another to imply that Heaven initiates those deaths; one thing to argue that Heaven, by its immutable laws, directs what happens, another to imply that Heaven determines what happens. Paradoxically, Hamlet's qualification or justification of the results of his own action in ascribing them to disparate forces beyond his control stresses his habitual rejection of forces outside the self.

By the last act not only has Hamlet's adoption of the practice of seeming been a futile revenge that "swoopstake . . . draw[s] both friend and foe"—four people dead who had nothing to do with the original crime; the noble Laertes willing to give "both the worlds . . . to negligence" (IV.v.134); "the people muddied, / Thick and unwholesome in their thoughts" (81–82); Claudius, grown larger in villainy, still on the throne—but it has also brought about his own defeat, his alienation from reason and reality. And Shakespeare allows us no doubt that this alienation follows on a willful choice of *show*. We have seen that Hamlet's use of theater is defined by the dumb show and violence that his production immediately reproduces. The King's conscience may be "caught" by the dramatic enactment of his crime (as by any reminder of it); but, like the offense, such "action" produces only grief. Conscience is not "moved" to an implementation of remedy. And when Hamlet's arrival at the prayer scene gives Hamlet another opportunity—fortuitous or the "assay" of angels?—to put into practice an action antithetical to *show*, he rejects it.

If, at this moment, he had employed the accent of a Christian or the action of a man (as he has defined that action); if he had practiced the philosophy so recently urged on Polonius; if, supplementing the King's attempt to "look up," he had said what he is soon to say to Gertrude, "Repent what's past"—perhaps he could have effected repentance in Claudius and, thus, forgiveness in the Ghost. For Hamlet is the middle man between the "man" who cannot forgive and the man who cannot repent. But although Hamlet sees that " 'tis heavy with [the King]" (III.iii.84), he has used dumb show and play, not to "give [Claudius] some light," but rather to elicit a revelation of darkness.[16] His secret intent fittingly produces a secret declaration of offense; and like Hamlet, Claudius persists in public dumbness. Moreover, the King's dumb show elicits from Hamlet a revelation of darkness. The willfulness of Hamlet's determination on a reprisal in excess of Claudius's crime, his decision to try to destroy soul as well as body,[17] is underlined when he later answers Laertes' "The devil take thy soul" with the judgment, "Thou pray'st not well" (V.i.281–82). Species of *show* do indeed lead "presently" to species of proclamation that reveal the "malefactor." And again we see, in this ironic issue, the motif of "purposes . . . Fall'n on the inventors' heads."

IV

One suspects that Shakespeare might say, " 'Who, that's but [a critic], fair, sober, wise,' would find Hamlet's shortcoming in his delay in killing Claudius?" For Shakespeare nowhere suggests that the time would have been put in "joint" if Hamlet had ascended the throne by killing the King. The corruption in Denmark, by evidence of the words of the gravedigger, begins before King Hamlet's murder; and a contributing factor to that disorder is king-killing. Shakespeare makes no case for martial retribution or revenge in the actions of Laertes and Fortinbras, and such counterpart to Hamlet's cause does not, however disparate the circumstances, afford a perspective that puts any desire for revenge in a favorable light. Nor, in this play, does Shakespeare proffer any brief for the use of arms: even the sport of dueling is made suspect when Hamlet uses the word *violence* to describe it (V.ii.309). One suspects, too, that Shakespeare would be startled at those critics who take a small step beyond finding Hamlet's fault in his lack of bloodthirstiness, to taking him for their moral arbiter in all matters, despite his bloodthirstiness. Because Hamlet returns from his sea voyage uttering, as always, fine principles like "There's a divinity that shapes our ends" (10), "There's a special providence in the fall of a sparrow" (230–31), and "The readiness is all" (233), we are surely not intended to overlook their unconscious irony in the context of his deeds and find him regenerated or converted,[18] despite the revealed contrast between his faith and the faith of the First Clown, that other and "absolute" gravedigger; the irrational ranting over Ophelia's grave; the ruthless self-justification for the murder of his former schoolfellows; the callous treatment of Laertes; the hypocritical and superfluous elaboration on the lie about the death of Polonius. Even his apparently inconsequential words to Laertes and Claudius about his "ignorance" and weakness in dueling (266–72) are suggestive: Shakespeare does not have him thus directly contradict what he has just said to Horatio (220–22), in order to stress his courtesy, but rather to reveal how meaninglessly he pledges "by this hand" (269;cf.III.ii.349), how needlessly he lies, how easy a property he now finds *seeming*. And if one insists that such details are unimportant, one is still left with the uncompromising fact that he eventually murders as savagely as Claudius without the subsequent sense of guilt that plagues Claudius. Such a parallel and such a contrast do not show that he is incapable of pitiless and violent action or that he is Heaven's "minister," however he may censure or glorify his own conduct.

In the face of the "havoc" at the end of the play, one must take into account the burden of the figurative design and the conceivable effect of a practice antithetical to *show*. An open and direct declaration of Claudius's guilt, an appeal to repentance, an attempt to administer a judgment that (not excusing or extenuating the evil) is positive, rather than negative—all may appear, given Claudius's position and nature, and only the accusation and evidence of a Ghost, eminently unrealistic. But the rub in our acceptance of such a course is not in its peril or its futility, not in the character of Claudius, but in the character of Hamlet and in ourselves. Shakespeare denies its material impracticability by reiterations about the people's regard for Hamlet and by the revelation of Claudius's weak hold on the throne when Laertes, with the help of the rabble, "o'er-bears [the King's] officers" (IV.v.101–2); he does not to no purpose change the situation found in the available sources of the story, where the courtiers connive at the uncle's treachery and tyranny. He also qualifies the quixotism in a premise that Claudius might be capable of repentance by giving him a disturbed conscience, by allowing for a goodness still resident in him, and by insisting on the constructive force of noble action. It is characteristic of Shakespeare to plead the case of faith and charity while demonstrating the obstacles to their practice, and in other plays he shows such qualities accomplishing more remarkable reversals than repentance in Claudius would be. Moreover, the difficulty of imagining a profitable response to an act does not refute the wisdom of the act itself. But though events suggest that there would be little danger for Hamlet in such a course and that it might elicit penitence in the King, Hamlet does not transmute his loftiest beliefs into literal practice. And the reader is tempted to share in Hamlet's rejection of his own preachment that merit lies in "bounty," that treating a man according to his desert is not equivalent to using him "after [one's] own honour and dignity." For quite aside from whether Hamlet, with a "dear father" slain and with engrained notions of knightly honor and justice, could actualize such an ideal as he enjoins on Polonius, the reader tends to reject it as impractical (if he considers it at all), as an inadequate, foolish, vain, soft response to great human evil and the "realities" of the human condition. Even as we see the effect of Hamlet's rejection of his better knowledge, even as we perceive "in passages of proof" that "Lilies that fester smell far worse than weeds," Claudius's easy and immediate decision to kill Hamlet is in such contrast to Hamlet's agonized delay in killing Claudius that our emotional identification with Hamlet is reinforced and we *feel* that Claudius is a villain and Hamlet, whatever he has become, is not and that, all pretty principles aside, villainy should get its "desert." Thus, Shakespeare challenges commitment to, and faith in, a conception of justice that man professes to revere.

But while he brings home to us the difficulty in giving the decision "to be" more than lip service, he does not evade or dilute the effect of wrong choice, the decision "not to be." It is hard not to mislead oneself about Hamlet when other characters in the play, the circumstances of his death, and the echoes of an original greatness of mind all speak for him. But one must not be misled by the estimate that even the man who plots his death has of him as one "most generous and free from all contriving": the ghosts of Rosencrantz and Guildenstern would find such a description inexact. One must not be misled into thinking that he does not make a choice, does not act on the Ghost's injunction, simply because he does not immediately take a particular kind of action: if it is true that "on his choice depends / The sanity and health of this whole state" (I.iii.20–21), then the fact that Denmark is increasingly given over to insanity and sickness indicates a failure of choice. One must not be misled by the sympathy one feels for him as the victim of Claudius's and Laertes' treachery: if he can reword what he has called the "fortune" of an "intruding fool" into "I have shot mine arrow o'er the house, / And hurt my brother," then his own disregard for truth characterizes "this brother's wager" (III.iv.31–32; V.ii.254–55,264). One must not be misled by the displays of nobility that he is still capable of, any more than one is misled by Claudius's displays of honesty, pity, and concern into calling him a "good and gentle king." In the scene in the graveyard where we fittingly find Hamlet at the opening of the last act, we can hardly be less appalled by the change in the Prince who originally put on the "antic disposition" than he is by the remains of Yorick, that other "fellow of infinite jest, of most excellent fancy" (V.i.203–4). Hamlet has gone to the water, "a sore decayer" (188).

He may later respond to Laertes' forgiveness with forgiveness and, though Laertes has been as treacherous in his use of poison as Claudius had been in killing King Hamlet, do what the Ghost has not done. But the Ghost has not been confronted with repentance; and though one should not underestimate Hamlet's reaction to Laertes' request, neither should one allow sympathy for Hamlet and the conviction that *he* could never have resorted to Laertes' particular brand of perfidy, to obscure Laertes' magnanimity and, in this play, its importance. Unlike Claudius, Laertes repents; unlike the Ghost, he forgives; and he does not wait to know that Hamlet is "desirous to be bless'd" before begging "blessing." In short, it is Laertes who, though he has lost both father and sister, manages the difficult action. Hamlet immediately responds with pardon, but there is still no indication in his words that he has any real awareness of his own wrongdoing. Yet, in a way, though his knowledge that Laertes has had "cause" to feel "wrong'd" may bear on his readiness to forgive, his lack of a true sense of transgression or contrition accentuates his generosity. Thus, at the conclusion of a tragedy brought about, in part, by a failure to exercise faith in men's good, whatever their evil, we see proof, not only of a virtue still resident in corrupted men, but also of the potency of the virtuous act. Hamlet, not conscience-stricken like Laertes (or, earlier, Claudius), retains a nobility that can be sparked by a noble action. But it is his general departure from goodness that gives point to his response.

Finally, one must not be misled by Horatio's estimate of Hamlet. Horatio exclaims over Hamlet's dead body, "Flights of angels sing thee to thy rest!" But though he invokes a singing, the next line that Shakespeare gives him is, significantly, "Why does the drum come hither?" (V.ii.371–72). It is a "speaking" that is put in motion for Hamlet: the "rites of war / Speak loudly for him" (410–11); the "peal of ordnance" marks his passage to his rest. Those readers who accept Horatio's view of Hamlet are likely to assume that the story Horatio promises to tell is essentially *Hamlet*, the story they have heard. One critic says, "What is there to be told? No more than we . . . have just lived through in our imagination with the poet."[19] One must add, "Not nearly so much." Horatio is not privy to all that Shakespeare gives us. For example, he has not heard the First Clown's answer to the riddle about the strongest builder: "When you are asked this question next, say 'a grave-maker:' the houses that he makes last till doomsday" (V.i.65–67). Hamlet has made at least five such houses; and according to the Clown, the man who digs a grave for another man, digs his own (133–34). If the implications in the allusion to doomsday are not to be scanted, if there are here "necessary question[s] of the play . . . to be considered," then Shakespeare's view of Hamlet is not Horatio's.

Moreover, what Horatio will "deliver" is, by evidence of his own words, only an account of "acts" that are imaged in "such a sight as this" (V.ii.397,392,412), the sight that horrifies Fortinbras and the English Ambassadors. Horatio proposes a narrative replete with a kind of "dumb show": "high on a stage" the dead bodies will "be placed to the view" (389), and he will play the presenter when this is "perform'd" (404), explaining this show with an account "of carnal, bloody, and unnatural acts, / Of accidental judgments, casual slaughters, / Of deaths put on by cunning and forced cause, / And, in this upshot, purposes mistook / Fall'n on the inventors' heads" (392–96). But, at the risk of belaboring the obvious, one must note that Horatio is no more aware of the large significance of his own language in speaking of "acts," of death "put on," of "this upshot," than he is of the figurative burden of Fortinbras's words when, in a language charged with imagery that throughout the play defines the nature of *show*, the Norwegian speaks of the "feast" that these trappers and shooters now shadow forth as the "quarry" that "death . . . at a shot / So bloodily hast struck" (375–78). Obvious distinctions aside, if one accepts the notion that Horatio will approximate what "we have just lived through," one is missing the distinction between show and play, on stage or off.

We see in Horatio's own summary of the action the boundaries of his proposed narrative and dramatic presentation: violence and death, the matter of the mute scene "high on a stage," will be his theme. If Shakespeare's play "hold[s], as 't were, the mirror up to nature" and shows "the very age and body of the time his form and pressure," then one can hardly find in a silent scene that mirrors only death a facsimile of *Hamlet*, however apt its commentary. Such a lifeless show as Horatio projects has counterpart in Hamlet's dumb show; and such a narrative, counterpart in the speech of the First Player (though now the "cue for passion" *is* a subjective one). Those critics who would find in Horatio's promised show the gist of *Hamlet*, and in his promised account of a story of revenge the essence of *Hamlet*, are identifying one aspect of Shakespeare's play with the whole play. Nor is the effect *within* the play of actions described in an imagery of theater the effect of *Hamlet*. Shakespeare's influence on his audience will be the subject of my concluding remarks; the effect of Horatio on *his* audience is projected by the logic of the figurative design: those who watch the duel, which Hamlet characteristically calls "this chance," are "but mutes or audience to this act" of noise and violence that results in "silence" and senseless ears; and we cannot suppose that anything more than a similar dumbness will be effected by the "dumb show" high on a stage and a narrative that mirrors only that silent scene.

Any other issue is denied by the insistent use, here at the end of the play, of the elements of the *show* symbolism and the strict adherence to the premises of the figurative pattern. Shakespeare ends other plays with the bearing offstage of the dead to the sound of a dead march; but in *Hamlet* he also employs the noise of the ordnance to mark the action.[20] The use of the guns, like the forecast of a mute scene to succeed the noise of the funeral procession, invests the conclusion of *Hamlet* with a peculiar pessimism. Again, in this continuation of the process depicted throughout the play, we are told that dumb show and noise follow on dumb show and noise; more particularly, we are told that there is no real change in Denmark. The consequence of the choice of the ruling house of Denmark is manifest, not just in the death of its representatives, but also in the triumph of the guns and the "prophesy" of the election of the militarist Fortinbras, who, most suggestively, has the sanction of a "dying voice" (366–67). Fortinbras may possess admirable qualities and instincts; he may say that the sight he sees "shows much amiss" in court, but it is a show he likes: it "becomes the field" (412–13). His allegiance is to the custom, the ceremony, the "rites of war"; the noise he glorifies is the "warlike volley" (with which he honors the messengers bearing the news of the death of Rosencrantz and Guildenstern) and the "soldier's music" (with which he honors the Prince for whom Horatio has invoked the singing of angels). He may have earlier accepted the arrests and rebukes of his uncle; but he is a man of ambition (I.ii.21;IV.iv.49), and he wastes no time in declaring a "claim" to "rights" in Denmark (V.ii.401–2). Given what we know of the character of Fortinbras, we can have little doubt that now, as at the beginning of *Hamlet*, "nightly [will toil] the subject of the land, / [With] daily cast of brazen cannon, / And foreign mart for implements of war" (I.i.72–74). Hamlet's giving his "voice" to Fortinbras may appear to resolve the attitudes crystallized in the compact of their fathers, and it may appear a fitting sequel to Fortinbras's giving over his "pester[ing] . . . message" and accepting rule. But the prospect of a speech "from [a dead] mouth whose voice will draw on" the election of Fortinbras (V.ii.403) subtly and ironically echoes the beginning of *Hamlet*. And the prospect of a show with a "presenter" who will tell of "acts" of violence (and will no more deal in positive values than did that earlier presenter who was called "as good as a chorus," [III.ii.255]) intensifies that echo and reinforces the implication that Denmark will not escape, in this new representative of its "voice," the treadmill of noise and dumbness.

That "the cease of majesty . . . is a massy wheel" is, thus, ironically implied in the accession of Fortinbras. For one must feel the loss to Denmark when a Hamlet, the "courtier's, soldier's, scholar's, eye, tongue, sword" (III.i.159), gives way to a Fortinbras, all soldier, all sword. One must sense the "boisterous ruin" (III.iii.22) that attends on the waste of great capacities for the public good when "eye, tongue, sword" (the proper order) are as misapplied in fact as they are in the analogy of Ophelia's order—courtier, soldier, scholar. In the somber echoes, in the final scene, of the figurative comment throughout the drama, one hears the long reverberations of Prince Hamlet's choice of noise and dumb show when it is manifested—not only in the scene of carnage, the noise of the guns, and the prospect of *show*—but also in his giving his "voice" to Fortinbras, and Denmark to the rule of a man who "find[s] quarrel in a straw" (IV.iv.55).

In the light of image and symbol, the pattern in Hamlet's tragedy is clear: the poison poured into his ears works, and he becomes corrupted and corrupter, trapped and trapper. Rejecting the higher rule he is aware of, he limits himself to the dungeon of self. Choosing to cover himself with the crust of madness and to set a mousetrap with the bait of falsehood, he is caught in his own toil and falls into seeming—"quite, quite down" (III.i.162). Making the decision for death, he is subject to that choice: his existence becomes a matter of "dumb-show and noise," ominously "the rest . . . silence." He has called Claudius "a thing . . . Of nothing" (IV.ii.30–32),[21] a phrase that, if Shakespeare's figurative and thematic comment holds, also eventually describes Hamlet, for he has chosen "not to be."

But here one pauses. One may believe that those critics who allow Hamlet's rhetoric to lead them to disregard, extenuate, or justify his wrongdoing are, with him, making morality and religion "a rhapsody of words" (III.iv.47–48) and, with Horatio, confusing nothing with something. One may believe that arguments that Hamlet is Heaven's minister to scourge Denmark of evil or a scapegoat whose sacrifice ensures the public good are narrowing the scope of Shakespeare's representation of evil. One may believe it absurd to contend that though Shakespeare insists on the boomerang of violence and the futility of revenge, he intends us to ascribe men's violent and vengeful actions to Hell in some instances, and to Heaven in others; or that though men who "would circumvent God" (V.i.87), who send a fellow to death "unhousel'd," or who consign a human soul to the Devil are to be censured, such censure applies only to Claudius and Laertes, not to Hamlet. Nevertheless, one must also concede that the feeling behind efforts to put Hamlet's actions in a favorable light is a valid response to the drama. The great range of critical reaction to Hamlet's character—from those who find him ever the "sweet prince" to those who find him "a poison"—stems from apparently contradictory demands that Shakespeare makes on his audience. On the one hand, there is the logic of the figurative and factual pattern: we are told that the monster, custom, can consume the noblest substance and that a habitual use of false-seeming can blast the most sovereign reason; we are shown the disintegration of a man who, despite the most remarkable gifts, chooses to imitate humanity abominably and whose own criteria for human excellence gauge his descent into silence. On the other hand, even as Shakespeare explicates and depicts Hamlet's ruining from good, he holds our pity and sympathy, even our loyalty, for Hamlet. The resolution of these pulls is not to be found in refusing to acknowledge one of them; and the fact that the thesis developed in this study accommodates them both is an uncommon point in its favor. It supports the proposal that by two demands, one on a sense that does not blink at evil done and one on a sensibility that does not find justice in taking only evil into account, Shakespeare extends his comment on Hamlet's judgment of Claudius; and effecting what he has been saying is an aim of art, he leads his audience to exercise a judgment that does not "o'er-step."

He may employ drama to mirror the particular and the general consequences of unleashing and serving the forces of evil; he may admit of no defeat of those forces in the promise of *show* and the accession of a prince who glories in *noise*. His conclusions about the society he pictures may be somber: to flawed man, the singing of angels is a dream; the "reality," the choice he implements, is the sound of the drum and the peal of the ordnance, worldly honor, power, pomp. From Francisco's "I am sick at heart" in Act I to Hamlet's "Thou wouldst not think how ill all 's here about my heart" in Act V and from the Ghost's concern over the wrong done him to Hamlet's dying concern for himself, his "wounded name," one may hardly avoid saying with Ophelia, "O, how the wheel becomes it!" From the Ghost's begging a hearing to Horatio's begging a hearing, one may hardly avoid saying with Hamlet (as he responded to the *Prologue's* "We beg your hearing patiently"), "Is this . . . the posy of a ring?" With recurrent phrases about foul practice that turns on itself, arrow that reverts to bow, engineer hoist with his own petard, purposes fallen on inventors' heads; with descriptions, early and late, of a succession of sounds that reverberate from heaven; with a dramatic process wherein dumbness and noise inevitably and repeatedly lead to dumbness and noise—Shakespeare may hardly allow us to avoid the melancholy conclusion that the futile and monotonous round of evil is not, in this play, halted. But, nevertheless, in holding the mirror up to a nature that reflects an individual and a general human failure, Shakespeare images good as well as evil. And although *Hamlet* is a drama about a time whose age and body are mirrored in the form and pressure of dumb shows and noise, Shakespeare leads his audience to reflect "true play."

He uses theater to beget a temperance toward a Prince whose cruelty and treachery cannot be gainsaid and a people whose prizing of dross is undeniable. If both the glorification of ugly fact and the judgment that rests solely on fault are productive and reflective of dumb shows and noise, then Shakespeare encourages us to neither an evasive renaming of evil nor a swinish nicknaming on the basis of it, to neither a denial that Hamlet becomes a "bloody . . . Remorseless, treacherous . . . villain" nor an assertion that he can be summed up in words like *villain* or *beast*. Whatever else Hamlet does, he finds it hard to kill a King and kinsman; and whatever he becomes, he finds it easy to forgive his own killer. The point of such differences from Claudius and the Ghost is not that Hamlet is less the murderer. (After all, Claudius's uneasy conscience, in contrast to Hamlet's remorselessness, makes the King no less a fratricide; and the Ghost's admission that murder in the best is most foul, in contrast to Hamlet's refusal to see foulness in the murder of his former friends, makes the Ghost no less the revenger.) The point is simply that judgment cannot rest on an extenuation of evil or a discounting of good. Professor Ornstein says that "Shakespeare creates within us a sympathy with Hamlet which becomes almost an act of faith,"[22] and this seems to me a perceptive observation as it applies to both a common reaction and to Shakespeare's intention; but that sympathy does not derive "primarily from what [Hamlet] says rather than what he does."[23] Much of what Hamlet says—particularly in the last act—is as twisted as his deeds, and one deed is better than anything he says. However, even as Hamlet stands a gravemaker among graves, even as his words and deeds reflect corruption, he still can stir our minds to admiring wonder; even grown inhuman, he still can stir us to laughter with a human, humorous amusement at Osric's nonsense (and there is nothing like a sharing of laughter to temper adverse opinion of another); even in the midst of a havoc that his words and deeds have helped to bring about, he still can stir us to approval with his response to Laertes' plea. Shakespeare tells us that corrupted by *seeming*, Hamlet is still capable of words and actions antithetical to *show*, as are other representatives of this noisy age. But the significance of our acceptance of this is importantly dependent on our cognizance of an individual and general decay.

For Shakespeare thus elicits from us a response that enforces the argument he has been developing in his show/play symbolism and leads us to affirm its validity. The further parted from reason and rule Hamlet is shown to be, "the less [he] deserve[s]" in conjunction with the willingness of the audience to "take [him] in" on the strength of a good incommensurate to his evil, "the more merit is in . . . bounty" and the less that audience can argue that giving bounty to the sinner is "unrealistic." Hamlet has said that if a man is used "after his desert . . . who should 'scape whipping?" Shakespeare has demonstrated repeatedly, in the choices of an extravagant and erring Prince and society, that if judgment reflects only evil and false-seeming, "who should 'scape [dumb shows and noise]?" And he makes us bear witness to the choice that redounds to every man's good, and to the reality of a remarkable work of art. Accomplishing what it argues, *Hamlet* leads us to testify to its truth: by exercising a conception of justice that includes a temperance, a charity, a faith in a man's nobility despite his manifest evil, one imitates "great creating nature" and mirrors the reality that "passeth show."

Notes

Chapter One

1 *What Happens in "Hamlet"* (Cambridge, 1935), p. 145.

2 *Form and Meaning in Drama* (London, 1956), p. 306.

3 III.ii.14–15. The text cited is *The Complete Works of Shakespeare,* ed. Hardin Craig (Chicago, 1961); hereafter cited as *Works.*

4 Frances A. Foster, "Dumb Show in Elizabethan Drama before 1620," *Englische Studien* 44 (1911): 10 n. And see B. R. Pearn, "Dumb-Show in Elizabethan Drama," *RES* 11, no. 44 (October 1935): 403. An excellent recent study, which includes comment on the show in *Hamlet,* is Dieter Mehl's *The Elizabethan Dumb Show* (London, 1965). Chapter 2 of the present study makes frequent reference to Professor Mehl's findings.

5 Space does not permit a separate documentation of each of the following interpretations, some of which are found in many articles and books. My synthesis of critical comment on the dumb show includes a number of studies dealing primarily or in some detail with the play scene: W. W. Greg, "Hamlet's Hallucination," *MLR* 12, no. 4 (October 1917): 393–421, and "The Mouse-Trap—a Postscript," *MLR* 35

(1940): 8–10; W. W. Lawrence, "The Play Scene in *Hamlet*," *JEGP* 18 (1919): 1–22, and "Hamlet and the Mouse-Trap," *PMLA* 54, no. 3 (1939): 709–35; Henry David Gray, "The Dumb-Show in *Hamlet*," *MP* 17, no. 1 (May 1919): 51–54; W. J. Lawrence, "The Dumb Show in *Hamlet*," *Life and Letters* 5 (November 1930): 333–40; Wilson, *What Happens in "Hamlet,"* pp. 138–63; Levin L. Schücking, *The Meaning of "Hamlet,"* tr. Graham Rawson (Oxford, 1937), pp. 128–32; J. M. Nosworthy, "A Reading of the Play-Scene in *Hamlet*," *ES* 22 (1940): 161–70; C. J. Sisson, "The Mouse-Trap Again," *RES* 16, no. 62 (1940): 129–36; A. Hart, "Once More the Mouse-Trap," *RES* 17, no. 65 (1941): 11–20; Moody E. Prior, "The Play Scene in *Hamlet*," *ELH* 9 (1942): 188–97; J. H. Walter, "The Dumb Show and the 'Mouse Trap,'" *MLR* 39 (1944): 286–87; Harley Granville-Barker, *Prefaces to Shakespeare* (Princeton, N.J., 1946), 85–93; Richard Flatter, *Hamlet's Father* (London, 1949), pp. 40–59; Andrew J. Green, "The Cunning of the Scene," *ShQ* 4 (1953): 395–404; Sara Ruth Watson, "The 'Mousetrap' Play in *Hamlet*," *N&Q* 200 (1955): 477–78; John P. Emory, "The Dumb-Show in *Hamlet*," *N&Q* 205 (1960): 77–78; Mehl, *The Elizabethan Dumb Show*, pp. 110–20.

6 But see Flatter, *Hamlet's Father*, pp. 47–51.

7 *What Happens in "Hamlet,"* pp. 158–60.

8 "Hamlet's Hallucination," pp. 401–7. Greg modifies this argument in "The Mouse-Trap—a Postscript."

9 Here I do not, of course, use the term in its technical sense. See Bertram Joseph, *Conscience and the King* (London, 1953), pp. 30–32, for a similar use of the expression in its meaning of a mute exhibition of melancholy, grief, or passion.

10 E.g., the "solemn march." Traditional uses of the convention will be discussed in Chapter 2 of this study.

11 See, e.g., Wilson, *What Happens in "Hamlet,"* pp. 153, 155, and A. Hart, "Once More the Mouse-Trap," p. 12. Wilson cites the discrepancy to support his argument that the dumb show comes as an unwelcome surprise to Hamlet. But that Hamlet censures dumb shows proves nothing about the nature of the play he commissions: quite aside from the fact that his speech and action are often at odds, his taste in drama is not the basis for his selection of *Gonzago*. And his allusion to dumb shows could well have stemmed from his preoccupation with the impending performance and the incidental knowledge that it contained a mime. Lacking proof to the contrary, one is safer in assuming that *Gonzago* contained a dumb show when Hamlet first saw it than in conjecturing that it did not. But such an assumption still leaves one with the puzzling fact that Shakespeare selects this particular stage convention as one of the objects of Hamlet's scorn.

12 *The Dream of Learning* (Oxford, 1951), pp. 42–43.

13 *Shakespeare's Imagery* (Cambridge, 1935), pp. 75–78, 328–29. She speaks of Shakespeare's habit of seizing on "sound . . . as abhorrent"; of his tendency to connect noise with chaos, war, evil; of his use of "echoing and re-echoing sound" to emphasize the "boundless effects of evil."

14 It is on Hamlet's forecast of the stage wooing that Claudius rises. Since Hamlet later refers to the King's reaction "upon the talk of the poisoning," it is often assumed that Lucianus's speech or Hamlet's "He poisons him i' the garden for 's estate" occasions the King's departure. But the court knows of the wooing; it does not know of the poisoning. And whatever Claudius's reaction to the talk of poisoning, the talk of wooing "moves" him.

15 When Ophelia sees the dumb show, she says, "What means this, my lord?" and Hamlet answers, "Marry, this is miching mallecho; it means mischief" (III.ii.148–49). The words *miching mallecho* are usually glossed "sneaking mischief." The printing *mallecho* (*Malicho* in the First Folio, *Mallico* in the Second Quarto) results from the supposition of Malone and subsequent editors that the word originates in the Spanish *malhecho* ("misdeed"); though the OED says that there is no evidence that the Spanish word was familiar in English in Shakespeare's time, J. Dover Wilson says that it was current and ties "misdeed" to the "iniquity" of the players in introducing an "unauthorized" dumb show (*What Happens in "Hamlet,"* pp. 157–58). However, Hamlet says first what the show *is* and then what it *means,* and it *is* more properly and simply a "bad echo" of Claudius's evil deed than itself "mischief" or "misdeed," though the context accommodates any one of the meanings. *Miching,* in all of its denotations, applies more aptly to "echo" than to the other glosses of *mallecho*: it means both "skulking" and "playing truant," and all three mean "neglecting duty" (the meaning Shakespeare evokes in *Henry IV,* Part I, [II.iv.450], when Hal is called a *micher*). Thus, in calling the dumb show a "miching" bad echo of a murderous deed, Hamlet may suggest, not only the connotations "sneaking" or "lurking," but also the "idleness" or "duty-shirking" of which he often accuses himself. Perhaps the commonest meaning of *miche* is "to pilfer,' a signification that has less applicability to "mischief" or "misdeed" than to "bad echo," since the latter is pilfered from the Ghost's account. Hamlet's "This is miching mallecho" seems to me illustrative of Shakespeare's method of charging his words with several meanings; and I do not here seek so much to insist on any one interpretation as to point to hitherto unconsidered possibilities in the much-debated phrase if one reads *mallecho* as a play on "bad echo."

16 Craig, *Works,* p. 924 n.

17 The technique employed when the pressure of a dramatic action does not alter with an alteration in dramatic form obliquely reinforces the Ghost's puzzling incidental observation that the essential nature of murder does not change with the reason for it (murder is "most foul . . . in the best" [I.v.27]), and obliquely counters the frequent assumption of the *Hamlet* characters that the *stamp* of a deed changes with its form: in a drama where acts of killing are presumed to vary in their essence as in their shape or color, one is indirectly reminded that stopping another man's breath has its own unvarying character, whatever the circumstances.

18 "Hamlet and the Mouse-Trap," p. 710.

Chapter Two

1 *The Elizabethan Dumb Show,* pp. xii, 126–27, 184.

2 Ibid., pp. 22–23.

3 See ibid., p. 101.

4 Perhaps the marching of Fortinbras's soldiers, which H. Granville-Barker calls a "martial little pageant" (*Prefaces to Shakespeare,* p. 115), is intended to recall a form and subject matter of the dumb show and thus to add indirectly to the definition of "dumb show." Suggestively, the sight of this "pageant" leads Hamlet to the conclusion, "O, from this time forth, / My thoughts be bloody, or be nothing worth!" (IV.iv.65–66).

5 See Mehl, *The Elizabethan Dumb Show,* pp. 125–26.

6 Ibid., pp. 97–98, 93. Remarking on this characteristic of the mime, Mehl also says that "we have in *The Spanish Tragedy* that repetition which was typical of later dumb shows: the pantomime is immediately followed by explanatory narrative and the same events are presented twice in succession, the pantomime containing a typical gesture, while the narrative stresses the more individual part of the story and gives its general meaning" (p. 65).

7 Kitto, *Form and Meaning in Drama,* p. 264

8 See Mehl, *The Elizabethan Dumb Show,* p. 24.

9 Ibid., pp. 125, 133, 150, 153.

10 Ibid., p. 113. See also Foster, "Dumb Show in Elizabethan Drama before 1620," pp. 10–12, 16–17; Pearn, "Dumb-Show in Elizabethan Drama," pp. 388–95, 402–4; and Wilhelm Creizenach, *The English Drama in the Age of Shakespeare* (Philadelphia, 1916), p. 390.

11 See, e.g., Mehl, pp. 65–67, on the historical tableau in *The Spanish Tragedy,* "a short symbolic gesture" that is "chiefly directed . . . at the Spanish court being entertained by this performance."

12 John Cunliffe, "The Influence of Italian on Early Elizabethan Drama," *MP* 4 (1907): 601, noting that the Italians used the *intermedii* in both tragedy and comedy, says, "By confining the *dumb shows* to tragedy . . . the English courtiers gave them greater usefulness and significance." The remark may need some qualification, but it does demonstrate the close identification of the English dumb show with tragedy, even though shows appear in other kinds of drama.

13 Anne Righter, *Shakespeare and the Idea of the Play* (London, 1962), p. 160, says that in *Hamlet* the difference between reality and seeming is expressed in theatrical terms.

14 *Religio Medici and Other Works,* ed. L. C. Martin (Oxford, 1964), p. 74.

15 See Alice S. Venezky, *Pageantry on the Shakespearean Stage* (New York, 1951), p. 116.

16 *The Elizabethan Dumb Show,* p. 61.

17 *What Happens in "Hamlet,"* pp. 146–47.

18 *The Elizabethan Dumb Show,* p. 177 n.

Chapter Three

1 See, e.g., W. W. Lawrence, "Hamlet and the Mouse-Trap," *PMLA* 54, no. 3 (September 1939): 721–22. J. H. Walter, "The Dumb Show and the 'Mouse Trap,'" *MLR* 39 (1944): 286–87, says that this method of poisoning was "well known," but he cites no other use of, or reference to, it in drama aside from the single instance noted by Fredson T. Bowers in "The Audience and the Poisoners of Elizabethan Tragedy," *JEGP* 36 (1937): 501—Lightborne's speech in Marlowe's *Edward II* (V.iv.33–35). And, as Lawrence points out, the poison that Lightborne refers to is a powder, not a liquid. When Iago says, "I'll pour this pestilence into his ear" (*Oth.*II.iii.362), Shakespeare figuratively joins the properties of speech, liquid, and disease, as he does in *Hamlet,* and perhaps he assumes a commonplace knowledge of a literal mode of poisoning. But it remains an uncommon method of murder and one uncommon in drama.

2 Norman N. Holland, "The Dumb-Show Revisited," *N&Q,* 203 (May 1958): 191, commenting on the method of murder as "singular, if not symbolic," points to the suggestiveness of the poison's being poured into both ears.

3 Holland, who notes that the word *ear* appears twenty-five times in the play, observes that "the ear . . . links the complex of images and ideas associated with the body, disease, and poison to the play's frequent references to language" (ibid., p. 191). And J. Swart, "I know Not 'Seems': A Study of Hamlet," *REL* 2, no. 4 (1961): 60–76, links "the poison in the ear which we may now recognize as a symbol" with "protestations of constancy that will prove to be insincere" (p. 73). See also pages 74–75 in the fine essay by T. McAlindon, "Indecorum in *Hamlet,*" *Shakespeare Studies* 5 (Dubuque, Iowa, 1969): 70–96.

4 After I had written this—indeed, at a time when my manuscript was being submitted to colleagues for criticism—Maurice Charney's *Style in "Hamlet"* (Princeton, N.J., 1969), which contains comment on the word *blast,* appeared. Although he does not explore the significance of the speech imagery, he notes the connection between *blast* and "diabolic curse," as well as "the notions of disease, explosion, [and] annihilating wind" in the word (pp. 81–82).

5 G. R. Elliott, *Scourge and Minister* (Durham, N.C., 1951), p. 21, finds the fact that the speech on the "dram of eale" is stopped by the coming of the Ghost "full of dramatic suggestion."

6 The reference to the "mole of nature," like those to "the o'ergrowth of some complexion" and "the stamp of one defect," is a detail in a

pattern of allusion throughout the play to surface blemish or external manifestation of defect—e.g., loathsome crust, tetter, ulcer, kibe, blister, canker, imposthume, pox, etc. But as the latter may indicate internal corruption, the "mole of nature"—explicitly linked to intrinsic conditions of "birth"—is also a detail in a pattern of allusion to internal blemish, to a poison in the blood. M. M. Mahood, *Shakespeare's Wordplay* (London, 1957), p. 117, finds in the use of *mole* here "a nuance of 'something that undermines from within' as well as . . . surface blemish" and thus an echo of a "shadow meaning" here in the subsequent epithet "old mole." J. R. Lowell, "Shakespeare Once More," *North American Review* 106 (April 1868): 659, observes that there is "a kind of genealogical necessity" in Hamlet's character; and Maynard Mack, "The World of Hamlet," *Yale Review* 41 (1952): 518, says that "even in himself [Hamlet] feels the taint, the taint of being his mother's son; and that other taint, from an earlier garden." Such observations that Hamlet's nature has been affected by conditions of birth, both general and particular, are in line with implications in the "mole of nature" phrase and are reinforced by implications in the "old mole" epithet, which is charged, like the earlier phrase, with several meanings and which serves, in the context of events, to suggest the internal and the external operations of both nature and fortune.

7 Like other commentators on the passage, I refer here to its general meaning—that the small portion of evil infects the whole substance. But Hamlet does qualify this description of the operation of the "dram of eale": the noble substance *in the general censure* takes corruption. Thus, there is, in the line, a comment on speech and on the speaker who, forgetting the "infinite virtues," judges only from the "particular fault."

8 See Francis Fergusson, *The Idea of a Theater* (Princeton, N.J., 1949), pp. 112–27, on "ritual scenes" in *Hamlet,* and McAlindon, "Indecorum in *Hamlet,*" pp. 86–93, on the abuse of ceremony.

9 Kitto, convinced that Shakespeare "meant something" by the gunfire, questions its use in the first act and then says, "In a later scene we read: *Trumpets sound, and cannon shot off within.* More guns—and now we understand: Claudius is drinking again, and Gertrude drinks, and the drinks are poison" (*Form and Meaning in Drama,* p. 262). Kitto's persuasion that the gunfire serves as a symbolic representation of poisoning is supported by such phrases as "contagious blastments," in which critics often find an imagery of poison or disease and which links both with the sequential sounds of trumpet and cannon.

10 *Shakespeare's Imagery,* pp. 75–78, 160, 328–29.

11 The metaphorical pattern suggests that one must distinguish between the physical and the spiritual effects of both the literal and the abstract hebenon. Rosencrantz and Guildenstern die; and, in an age less convinced than Shakespeare's of a lesser importance in the physical consequence, testimony to their spiritual health may seem quibble. But it is surely not unimportant that Rosencrantz tries to turn the implication in Hamlet's sardonic remark about Polonius and that, unlike Polonius's hypothetical "Dansker" who "closes . . . in this consequence," neither of Hamlet's former schoolfellows on any occasion verbally echoes the spirit of the malice he hears.

Chapter Four

1 See, e.g., W. H. Clemen, *The Development of Shakespeare's Imagery* (Cambridge, Mass., 1951), p. 113, and Charney, *Style in "Hamlet,"* pp. 35–39, 76, 78. Charney has further comment on "the theme of secrecy and poison" (pp. 31–52) and "disease and physical impairment" (pp. 75–88).

2 But see Charney, *Style in "Hamlet,"* pp. 115–23, who finds in the confinement images comment on "man's finiteness and mortality" and on "his attempts to break out of all confining boundaries with 'thoughts beyond the reaches of our souls' " (pp. 114–15).

3 Harold C. Goddard, *The Meaning of Shakespeare* (Chicago, 1951), p. 374, says that "the metaphor Shakespeare uses for [an] upsurge of racial emotion" in *Hamlet* is "*water*—the oldest and most universal symbol for the unconscious." He later calls "the Water . . . just another name for the infernal forces" that "rush in . . . to possess man" (p. 383). I find nothing in Shakespeare's figurative references to *water* that supports the notion he uses it as a symbol for "the unconscious" and nothing in the play to suggest that revenge is not a matter of conscious choice. But Goddard's proposal that *water*, in *Hamlet,* symbolizes evil (though in need of qualification) is supported by the evidence of fact and figure. The elements, necessary for man's health and yet sometimes inimical to health, are potentially symbols for either good or evil. Thus, an element is figuratively employed as it fits particulars of plot and as an elemental attribute or action furthers argument. Details of the plot of *Hamlet*—the drowning of Ophelia, Hamlet's capitulation to the passion of revenge while on a sea voyage, his coming to terms with sea pirates—are suggestively combined with allusions to *flood* in descriptions of danger, violence, temptation (e.g., Hamlet is warned that the Ghost may "tempt [him] toward the flood," and Laertes, "in a riotous head," is like "the ocean, overpeering of his list"); and finally, in the First Clown's speech, a water symbolism explicates the question of choice. By this time, the key word *flood,* its suitability in a drama about the danger in excess, has been established.

4 The armor of Pyrrhus is given a figurative significance: see II. ii. 474–75.

5 For varying opinions on the nature of the Ghost, see Greg, "Hamlet's Hallucination," *MLR* 12 (1917): 393–421; Wilson, *What Happens in "Hamlet,"* pp. 52–86; Lily B. Campbell, *Shakespeare's Tragic Heroes* (Cambridge, Mass., 1930), pp. 120–28; Roy Battenhouse, "The Ghost in *Hamlet:* A Catholic 'Linchpin'?" *SP* 48 (1951): 161–92, and *Shakespearean Tragedy: Its Art and Its Christian Premises* (Bloomington, Ind., 1969), pp. 237–44; I. J. Semper, "The Ghost in *Hamlet:* Pagan or Christian," *The Month* 195 (1953): 222–34; L. C. Knights, *An Approach to "Hamlet"* (London, 1960), pp. 44–48; Sister Miriam Joseph, "Discerning the Ghost in *Hamlet,*" *PMLA* 76 (1961): 493–502; Paul N. Siegel, "Discerning the Ghost in *Hamlet,*" *PMLA* 78 (1963): 148–49; Eleanor Prosser, *Hamlet and Revenge* (Stanford, Calif., 1967), pp. 97–142; Robert H. West, "King Hamlet's Ambiguous Ghost," in *Shakespeare and the Outer Mystery* (Lexington, Kentucky, 1968), pp. 56–68; and M. A. Mason, "The Ghost in *Hamlet:* a resurrected 'paper,'" *Cambridge Quarterly* 3 (Spring 1968): 127–52.

6 Hamlet, who thus describes the Ghost to Gertrude (III.iv.135), refers to the Ghost's apparel; but since in a speech soon after, he speaks of "habit" in the sense of "use" or "custom" as "a frock or livery, / That aptly is put on" and since all of the earlier details on King Hamlet emphasize the latter's observance of martial custom, the phrase suggests several meanings, one of which I borrow here.

7 This speech, which presents a positive alternative to both blood revenge and passive endurance, has not received the attention it deserves. But see Harold Skulsky, "Revenge, Honor, and Conscience in *Hamlet,*" *PMLA* 85 (January 1970): 78–96. Hamlet's words here to Polonius should be taken into account in any consideration of certain questions that repeatedly exercise students of the play: whether the play adheres to the formula of revenge tragedy and treats the aristocratic code as valid; whether, given a tradition of the heir's legal right and moral responsibility to avenge a father's murder and, on the other hand, God's law forbidding private vengeance, Hamlet is faced with irresoluable moral dilemma; whether Hamlet is an individual settling a private score or an individual instrument of divine justice; whether Shakespeare poses, as the proper alternative to revenge, the Stoic ideal of enduring the vicissitudes of fortune.

8 *Shakespearean Tragedy* (London, 1904), pp. 97, 100.

9 Schücking, *The Meaning of "Hamlet,"* p. 124, says that Hamlet's instruction to the players "has practically nothing to do with the action"; and Virgil Whitaker, *The Mirror Up to Nature* (San Marino, Calif., 1965), p. 188, says, "All the instructions to the players, except that they play 'The Murder of Gonzago,' are, strictly speaking, unnecessary." But see Roy Battenhouse, "The Significance of Hamlet's Advice to the Players," in *The Drama of the Renaissance: Essays for Leicester Bradner,* ed. Elmer M. Blistein (Providence, R.I., 1970), pp. 3–26.

10 For example, he calls Claudius ape, pajock, paddock, gib, bat, vice of kings, cutpurse, king of shreds and patches; Polonius, fishmonger and old baby; the Ghost, old mole and true-penny; Rosencrantz and Guildenstern, sponges.

11 Harold S. Wilson, *On the Design of Shakespearian Tragedy* (Toronto, 1957), pp. 47–48, quotes these "disenchanted lines" in contrast to "Goethe's judgment: A lovely, pure, noble, and most moral nature, without the strength of nerve which forms a hero, sinks beneath a burden it cannot bear and must not cast away." Wilson adds, "If either view causes us a shudder of dissent—and Goethe's certainly causes me one—we can hardly deny the grain of truth that each contains."

12 *The Moral Vision of Jacobean Tragedy* (Madison, Wis., 1960). p. 235.

13 Fredson Bowers, "Hamlet as Minister and Scourge," PMLA 70 (1955): 744–45. One might more reasonably suppose that since during the day the Ghost undergoes a trial by fire in his prison-house, his "freedom" at night is a continuation of trial and also contains a potential for purge.

Chapter Five

1 G. Wilson Knight, *The Wheel of Fire* (London, 1949), pp. 35, 38.

2 In the phrase "Hillo, ho, ho" with which Hamlet is greeted after he first talks with the Ghost, there is an implied hawk-image, one that he picks up in his answer, "Hillo, ho, ho, boy! Come, bird, come" (I.v.115–16). Again, when he tells Claudius that he feeds on promises and adds, "You cannot feed capons so" (III.ii.99–100), he may—depending on whether *feed* or *capons* is stressed—be calling himself a cock, a most suggestive image if he does, indeed, apply it to himself.

And again, when the mad Ophelia, who appears to refer in her songs alternately to Hamlet and Polonius (e.g., "His beard was as white as snow, / All flaxen was his poll") and to bid them both farewell as if both were dead, sings, "They bore him barefaced on the bier . . . Fare you well, my dove" and "For bonny sweet Robin is all my joy. / . . . And will he not come again? / No, no, he is dead" (IV.v.195–96;164, 167;187,191–92), the word *dove,* shortly to be used by Gertrude for Hamlet, and the name "sweet Robin," which echoes the bird imagery, may be references to Hamlet.

3 Charney, *Style in "Hamlet,"* p. 66, draws this conclusion and suggests that Hamlet here distinguishes between himself ("the heron") and his former schoolfellows ("preying hawks").

4 Annotators, who note that "handsaw" is a corruption for *hernshaw* and that "hawk" is a tool like a pickax, appear to conclude that one must settle on one of the two categories for comparison. But whereas a sane man would compare birds *or* tools, a "madman" would make a "mad" comparison; and the double meaning in the words implements "a happiness that often madness hits on" (II.ii.212–13).

5 See Charney, *Style in "Hamlet,"* pp. 63–64.

6 Such a claim moves Edward Topsell, *The History of Four-Footed Beasts and Serpents and Insects* (London, 1658), reprinted with a new introduction by Willy Ley (New York, 1967), I, 388, to say, "I do utterly dissent from all them that hold opinion that the Mole or Want is of the kind of Mice."

7 Traditionally, the dog-image may be applied to ranters, as well as to deceivers. Topsell, *The History of Four-Footed Beasts,* I, 109, says, "The voice of a Dog, is by the learned interpreted a railing and angry speech." There are other occasions in the play where the dog-image is evoked for those who are, in some sense, false: Hamlet describes flatterers and opportunists in the lines: "Let the candied tongue lick absurd pomp . . . Where thrift may follow fawning" (III.ii.65,67). And when he says, "For if the sun breed maggots in a dead dog, . . . Let [Ophelia] not walk i' the sun" (II.ii.181,184), it would appear that his conviction of her falsity leads him to suggest the image for her.

8 "Porpentine" (I.v.20), "crab" (II.ii.207), "stricken deer" and "hart ungalled" (III.ii.282–83) are odd or oddly used instances of a description of men in beast imagery not cited in my text or elsewhere in footnotes. The passage in which the first appears is interestingly recalled in III.iv.121–22. The second appears in Hamlet's remark that Polonius "should be old as [Hamlet is], if like a crab [he] could go

backward." As in other of Hamlet's "mad" observations, it is hard to determine the point at which Hamlet's intended meaning stops and Shakespeare's begins. But conceding that *old,* rather than *young,* is the idiom and accepting the obvious meaning of the line, one still is struck by the apt and paradoxical suggestion of a figurative "oldness" that comes from going back rather than forward and by the echo of Ophelia's description of Hamlet's leaving her "with his head over his shoulder turn'd" (II.i.97). See Battenhouse, *Shakespearean Tragedy,* p. 252, for interesting comment on this point.

9 Topsell, *The History of Four-Footed Beasts,* I, 2, 394–95, 389, 391, 83.

10 Ibid., p. 355.

11 Of course, the comment in the beast-images varies. Some that Hamlet employs are inoffensive; one for himself is commendatory; but most of them are pejorative.

12 In I.ii.152–53, Hamlet modestly disclaims a likeness to Hercules. If later in V.i.314–15, there is a hint that he identifies himself with the son of Zeus, the evidence of an alteration in his character is reinforced.

13 See McAlindon, "Indecorum in *Hamlet,*" pp. 79–80, and Charney, *Style in "Hamlet,"* pp. 272–75. But see Nevill Coghill, "Shakespeare as a Dramatist," in *Talking of Shakespeare,* ed. John Garrett (London, 1954), pp. 46–47.

14 See Warren V. Shepard, "Hoisting the Enginer with His Own Petar," *SQ* 7 (1956): 281–85, for comment on the trapper-trapped motif.

15 Ezek. 16:49.

16 Polonius's accompanying description of "a savageness in unreclaimed blood, / Of general assault" (II.i.34–35) may be intended to recall Hamlet's description of the "vicious mole of nature." If so, unlike Hamlet, Polonius suggests that an inherited condition and the commonness of error, either in men or in young men, add up to excuse.

17 See, e.g., I.ii.237–39. Cf. III.i.7 and III.i.13–14.

18 II.ii.140–42. Cf. I.iii.126–31.

19 *Julius Caesar* IV.iii.98–99.

20 If Rosencrantz is distinguishing between question and demand ("He answered our questions sparingly, but our demands freely"), the only conversation we have heard between Hamlet and his former school-fellows sheds no illumination on the distinction, since Rosencrantz and Guildenstern have made no demands on Hamlet and have asked few questions, none directly to the point of Claudius's commission. Hamlet, on the other hand, has asked more than two dozen questions and has demanded "by the rights of [their] fellowship, by the consonancy of [their] youth, by the obligation of [their] ever-preserved love," that they be "even and direct" with him. One might say that *they* have been "niggard of question; but, of [Hamlet's] demands, / Most free in [their] reply." It might be argued that Rosencrantz is deliberately misrepresenting the facts to curry favor with the King by implying that he and Guildenstern are carrying out the spirit of the King's request or to obscure their inefficiency as sleuths. But it seems much more likely that the contradiction between the conversation we have heard and Rosencrantz's description of it (if we are not to suppose other unheard conversation in the interim) merely reflects a gentlemanly desire to put the whole matter in the best possible light and a response to what the speaker considers only a natural concern for the health of a kinsman and prince.

21 "The Mystery of *Hamlet*," *ELH* 30, no. 3 (September 1963): 207.

22 *Form and Meaning in Drama*, p. 335.

23 Bradley, *Shakespearean Tragedy*, p. 169.

24 *The Wheel of Fire*, pp. 316, 35.

25 See Leo Kirschbaum, "In Defense of Rosencrantz and Guildenstern," in *Two Lectures on Shakespeare* (Oxford, 1961), pp. 5–18, for intelligent comment on these two characters.

Chapter Six

1 For evidence of Shakespeare's firsthand familiarity with the *Aeneid*, see T. W. Baldwin, *William Shakspere's Small Latine & Lesse Greeke* (Urbana, Ill., 1944), 2:456–96. Fergusson, *The Idea of a Theater*, p. 140, says, "The anagoge, or ultimate meaning of the play, can only be

sought through a study of the analogical relationships within the play and between the world of Denmark and the traditional cosmos."

2 Virgil's Aeneas says, "The picture of my dear father came to mind / As I watched king Priam, a man of the same age, cruelly wounded, / Gasping his life away"; and he warns Anchises, "Pyrrhus is coming ... he loves / Butchering sons in front of their fathers, fathers at the altar" (*The Aeneid of Virgil,* trans. C. Day Lewis [London, 1952], pp. 47, 50). Since he portrays Pyrrhus as one who offends against age, family affections, and religion, the Virgilian hero's account of a king's death is a peculiarly appropriate choice for use in *Hamlet;* and the words of Shakespeare's Aeneas are reminiscent of the portrayal of Pyrrhus as a *father*-killer, as well as a king-killer: see, e.g., II.ii.480, 496. An omission in Shakespeare's version of the account of Priam's death is suggestive, particularly so if other versions are familiar to some part of his audience: unlike Virgil's Aeneas (or the Aeneas in Marlowe and Nashe's *The Tragedy of Dido, Queen of Carthage*), Shakespeare's Aeneas makes no explicit reference to Pyrrhus's slain father Achilles; one wonders whether Aeneas's outrage at Pyrrhus's "hellishness" in killing a father is thus given an element of the "particularity" that Hamlet finds in one instance of father-killing, but not in another.

3 Dido's husband, Sychaeus, is treacherously murdered (like Virgil's Priam "before the altar") by her brother Pygmalion, an intemperate "monster." Later, Sychaeus's ghost appears to Dido in a dream and discloses the truth about his death (see *The Aeneid of Virgil,* p. 20). Shakespeare's choice of Aeneas's tale may have been influenced by pertinent facts in the history of the hearer Dido: both she and Hamlet have experienced the grief attendant on such a deed as the one Aeneas describes, and both have a visitation from a ghost.

4 Virgil's Aeneas, in a notable passage, pauses, his movement of revenge against Turnus arrested when the latter pleads, " . . . if the thought of a father's / Unhappiness can move you—a father such as you had / In Anchises—I ask you, show compassion for aged Daunus, / And give me back to him." But after momentary indecision Aeneas—like Shakespeare's Pyrrhus after "pause"—sets to work with renewed fury (see *The Aeneid of Virgil,* pp. 287–88). In the *Aeneid* Pyrrhus does not pause; nor does he in *Dido, Queen of Carthage* before killing King Priam (see Clifford Leech, "The Hesitation of Pyrrhus," in *The Morality of Art* [London, 1969], pp. 41–49). The "wind" that occasions Priam's fall, the subsequent "crash" of Ilium, and the resultant "pause" of Pyrrhus appear to be details introduced into the story by Shakespeare (the questionable editorial emendation of *wound* to *wind* in Marlowe's play [II.i.254], to be based on Shakespeare's version). In ascribing arrested motion to the avenger, Shakespeare may have intended only to add another of the details linking Pyrrhus and Hamlet. But if, exploiting the particulars of a well-known passage wherein

Aeneas, after pause, refuses to pity a father, Shakespeare intensifies ironic undertones in his Aeneas's condemnation of Pyrrhus's ruthlessness, he also reinforces comment elsewhere in *Hamlet* on the mote in the eye of the avenger.

5 I depart here from my text: Craig follows the Globe text, based in this instance on the First Folio. In Q_2 the stage directions for the entrance of the Danish King and Queen are *Enter Trumpets and Kettle Drummes . . .* ; for the entrance of the Player King and Queen, *The Trumpets sounds. Dumbe show followes.* In F_1 the directions for the first entrance include *Danish March. Sound a Flourish;* for the second, they are *Hoboyes play. The dumbe shew enters.* The explicit call in the Second Quarto for a reiteration of the sound of trumpets serves a dramatic purpose, one that would have a striking impact if a director, by echoes in staging and action, were to underscore the implications in the juxtaposed entrances to the same sound. J. Dover Wilson, *The Manuscript of Shakespeare's "Hamlet" and the Problems of Its Transmission* (Cambridge, 1934), 2:182, says that the "superior authority" of the directions in the Second Quarto is "incontestable"; that "Q_2 [should be given] the preference when stage-directions differ"; but that omissions should be supplied "from F_1 where F_1 offers a plausible reading" (187). Directions in Q_2 for the stage use of trumpet, drum, and gun support, in every instance, my argument on both the general and the particular symbolic implications in the use of such noise: the pattern starts when a "Florish" marks both the entrance and the exit of King, Queen, and their Attendants in Act I and when in the same act the pomp and circumstance of "A florish of trumpets" and the noise of "2. peeces" mark the "rouse" of the King and his courtiers; in Act II again a Florish" heralds the entrance of the King and the Queen, and though nothing marks the entrance of the Ambassadors, significantly "A Florish" heralds the entrance of the Players; in Act III the implication in the juxtaposed entrances of the Danish rulers and the Play rulers to the sound of "Trumpets" is heightened by the fact that the first entrance of King, Queen, and Attendants in this act and at the beginning of Act IV is not accompanied by sound; in Act V "Trumpets" and "Drums" mark the entrance of "King, Queene, and all the state" and, during the fencing match, there are the directions (289, 292) *Trumpets the while* (not in F_1) and *Drum, trumpets and shot. Florish, a peece goes off.* Subsequent directions in F_1 are more detailed and suggestive: both F_1 and Q_2 direct that the far sound of a march mark the approach of Fortinbras (359,360); F_1, but not Q_2, calls for the entrance of Fortinbras "with Drumme" and contains the final stage direction, *Exeunt Marching: after the which, a Peale of Ordenance are shot off.*

6 This phrase comes from *Measure for Measure* I.iii.54.

7 "The World of Hamlet," *Yale Review* 41 (1952): 512.

8 See, e.g., III.i.53;IV.v.86;IV.vii.109;V.ii.78;II.ii.383–84;II.ii.502. When "painting" carries a different meaning, it is still used to figure forth falsehood, vanity, futility: the harlot employs a "plastering art" (III. i.51); women substitute "paintings" for the face God gives them (III.i. 148); Hamlet, as he looks at Yorick's skull and just before the advent of the mourners with Ophelia's body, says, "Let [my lady] paint an inch thick, to this favour she must come" (V.i.213–14).

9 See Charney, *Style in "Hamlet,"* pp. 137–53, on Shakespeare's "terms of art."

10 See Skulsky, "Revenge, Honor, and Conscience in *Hamlet,*" p. 82.

11 But see Battenhouse, "The Significance of Hamlet's Advice to the Players," p. 9, where he says, "Hamlet, after all, has the spirit of a Herod. The audience can thus enjoy . . . a kind of theater fare which [Hamlet's] aristocratic theory has forbidden." But has Hamlet forbidden Termagants and Herods (a particular stage fare) or overdone Termagants and out-heroded Herods (an acting style that does not hold to character)? The latter seems to me closer to what is actually said; but since Hamlet's words are ambiguous, I carefully record above what he does *not* specifically say. In arguing that Shakespeare does not endorse the theory expressed in Hamlet's advice, Battenhouse must narrow that advice to a particular meaning. Although he makes an admirable case for the contention that Hamlet's "views reflect canons typically neo-classical" (p. 6), it seems to me that in a play where a man repeatedly utters truths he denies or misapplies in action, one cannot say that that man's words comprehend *only* a meaning in line with his actions or tastes as elsewhere revealed. One may find in Hamlet's warning to the Players to avoid an excess that destroys illusion an implied dislike for a particular stage matter and in the rule that the play must show "the very age and body of the time his form and pressure" a sympathy for a "Jonsonian idea." But to say that if Hamlet did not violate his own rules (in his action as character), we would be stuck with "intolerable drama" is to ascribe to the violated rules only a special meaning—e.g., the rule of modesty that Hamlet violates does not refer to a general modesty Shakespeare admires but to a neoclassical "modesty" he censures. If some of Hamlet's words of advice accommodate a special interpretation, indirectly supplement Shakespeare's criticism of neoclassical drama, and help to characterize Hamlet's "view of life" as "melodramatic," it still seems to me that one must resort to special pleading to argue that Hamlet's advice does *not* also accommodate general truths that Shakespeare approves. And when Battenhouse finds in *Gonzago* and in the Player's Speech a mimicking by Shakespeare of styles of "underdone" and "overdone" writing, he appears to me to imply that Hamlet's advice *is* endorsed by Shakespeare, if the meanings Hamlet may have given his own words (as revealed by the dramatic insets) are not. The question of Shakespeare's

endorsement of Hamlet's advice aside, Battenhouse's argument indirectly provides significant reinforcement for the conclusions of my argument on the show/play symbolism.

12 *The Winter's Tale,* IV.iv.88.

13 *The Sermons of John Donne,* ed. Evelyn M. Simpson and George R. Potter (Berkeley, Calif., 1958), 9:75.

14 Craig, who inserts no word in line 169, notes that the line is "usually emended by inserting *master* after *either,* following Q_4 and early editors" (*Works,* p. 928 n). Other editors, with more attention to meter, insert *shame* or *curb.* But the logic of the whole passage, which points to custom, habit, use as "angel" *or* "devil," as well as the force of the immediate either-or construction and the sense of the words immediately preceding the defective line, suggests that Shakespeare may have written here some such word as "aid," "act," or "play," in *contrast* to "throw him out."

15 For comment on this line and on Hamlet's self-love, see Battenhouse, *Shakespearean Tragedy,* pp. 220–27, 234–37, 257–61; on his "self-centredness," Salvador de Madariaga, *On Hamlet* (London, 1948), pp. 103–7; on his "self-consciousness," Knights, *An Approach to "Hamlet,"* pp. 55–59. See also Robert B. Heilman's thoughtful essay, "To Know Himself: An Aspect of Tragic Structure," *REL* 5, no. 2 (April 1964): 36–57. Heilman says that "justification of self and blame of others are different sides of the same coin" and calls Hamlet "the most blame-prone of Shakespeare's heroes" (p. 49). He senses "two genres competing for the soul of one play: tragedy and melodrama. . . . Tragedy tries to make [Hamlet] a man of self-knowledge; melodrama tries to enclose him in the role of accuser that shuts out self-recognition" (p. 56).

16 Goddard, *The Meaning of Shakespeare,* pp. 360–62, says that there are two Hamlets; that "up to the play scene, the opposing natures in Hamlet are in something like equipoise" (p. 373); that it is "God's Hamlet" who chooses to put on a play (p. 362); that Claudius is "a fit subject for the redemptive power of art" (p. 364); that although Hamlet "has an opportunity to act like Shakespeare," he does not let the play "speak for itself," as Shakespeare would do (p. 364); that he makes "the right choice, but then . . . convert[s] an instrument of regeneration into an instrument of revenge (p. 382); that after the play, Claudius turns from "preparation for a fresh murder to repent the murder that has rendered this further one necessary" (p. 369). And Goddard asks, "If the mere fragment [of *Gonzago*] . . . could produce this de-

gree of repentance, what might the whole play, left to itself, have effected?" (p. 369). But whatever one might wish, Hamlet does not put on a play for the purpose of redemption or regeneration; and such implications in the label "God's Hamlet" for the dramatist Hamlet are not true to fact. Second, not only the intention of the dramatist but also the nature of the drama is, as *Hamlet* demonstrates, relevant to the effect of the drama. If Shakespeare argues that a play can be remedial, he obviously does not ascribe an uplifting or health-promoting force to all plays. And both the idea that a particular result in *Hamlet* is dependent on the presentation of a play and the idea that quantity (*Gonzago* enacted from start to finish) would enlarge that result are denied by the fact that an offhand remark by Polonius effects the kind of self-accusation Claudius expresses after the play-scene. Third, one can no more claim that Claudius's reaction to *Gonzago* is repentance than that Hamlet proposes to redeem him with the play. And when Goddard says that the two choices facing man are "art and war" (p. 382), he disregards his own perception elsewhere that art may be a kind of war. This is not to give Goddard's often suggestive and imaginative insights less than their due but rather to say that *he* sometimes shortchanges them.

17 These words have produced some extraordinary acrobatics from critics reluctant to confront Hamlet's savagery: e.g., one critic calls Hamlet's stated reasons for not killing Claudius "compunctions" and draws a contrast between him and an uncompunctious Laertes who declares himself willing "to cut [a] throat i' the church"; some of those most disposed to judging Hamlet only by his words arrive variously at the conclusion that *here* he does not mean what he says; another commentator takes a different tack: "Anyone who knows Elizabethan Literature ought to be aware that none of Shakespeare's contemporaries would have been greatly shocked by Hamlet's words." Censure of Hamlet's words and action in this scene is sometimes similarly nimble: one critic adds a refinement to the charge of remissness in dispatching the King—murder here, since Claudius is praying, would be "just and merciful"; another, overcome with a sympathy generated by Claudius's self-condemnation, scants the fact that the "kneeling figure grappling . . . with the problem of repentance" does not repent, and finds Claudius here "morally superior" to Hamlet. The scene is a touchstone to the critic's bias, subjectivity, insensibility, willingness to equivocate, or sentimentality. Essentially, it presents two instances of choice-making: Claudius opts to persevere in evil; Hamlet chooses to connive at a revenge beyond any shadow of condonation. Claudius has called for "light" and angel help—he is shown seeing, in the clearest light, his sins, the straits to which they have brought him, and the way out; yet he refuses to profit from the reason that tells him of repentance, "What can it not?" Hamlet happens by, conceivably providentially, and is made aware of the King's heaviness (quite a different matter from an awareness of only violence and treachery); and though his "scanning" it that the King will go to heaven if slain may show lack of knowledge of the King's spiritual condition, it shows an awareness of Heaven's rule for the repentant sinner. Yet he refuses to imitate the action he ascribes to God and resolves to circumvent (or to utilize for his own ends) the law that he acknowledges. Neither Claudius's retention of the "offence" in the face of a knowledge of heavenly justice nor Hamlet's cruelty and presumption in the face of a knowledge of heavenly mercy suggest that Shakespeare is pointing to either man's moral superiority. What he depicts is choice, choice made in defiance of a law that both choosers acknowledge. The ruthless action both men subsequently adopt is the inevitable concomitant of the choices made here. See John Vyvyan, *The Shakespearean Ethic* (London, 1959), pp. 138–39, for interesting comment bearing on this scene. A complexity in the matter of choice is suggested in an observation by Roy Walker, *The Time Is Out of Joint* (London, 1948), p. 95: Hamlet "is obsessed with hatred of evil, not love of goodness, and from hatred only hatred grows."

18 Many critics find Hamlet changed for the better after his sea voyage: e.g., he is "no longer in the tumult but above it"; he "has acquired some breadth of charity"; he is "become again the ideal prince." Such views are hard to reconcile with his conduct at Ophelia's grave. But whether one argues him changed for better or worse, he certainly remains unchanged in one respect: as before, he makes no move against Claudius; as before, he denounces the King only to Horatio. One can no longer adduce that he is incapable of prompt and ruthless action or that he has had no concrete proof of Claudius's perfidy. It would appear that Hamlet can be roused to murderous action only by immediate and overt challenge or threat to himself, as when he responds to the alarm raised by the hidden spectator in the Queen's closet, to the letter calling for his execution, or to Laertes' physical assault on him at the grave: " . . . take thy fingers from my throat; / For, though I am not splenitive and rash, / Yet have I in me something dangerous, / . . . hold off thy hand" (V.i.283–86).

19 Joseph, *Conscience and the King,* p. 50.

20 See n. 5 above.

21 Although I employ the common reading of the phrase, Hamlet's ambiguous reply ("The body is with the king, but the king is not with the body. The king is a thing . . . Of nothing") to Rosencrantz's words ("My lord, you must tell us where the body is, and go with us to the king") suggests that he may have the Ghost in mind, in which case his own words unintentionally and ironically provide even more illumination on the cause and nature of his own state. It would be characteristic of Hamlet to react against expressed regard for Claudius's kingly authority; to sieze an opportunity to remind his hearers, however obscurely, of his father; and to insist that Polonius *is* with the King, the dead King to whom body cannot be assigned, since he is "a thing . . . Of nothing" (the phrase recalls the use of *thing* to describe the Ghost).

22 *The Moral Vision of Jacobean Tragedy*, p. 235.

23 Ibid. In connection with Ornstein's comment above, I should like to draw attention to Kenneth Muir's "Imagery and Symbolism in *Hamlet*," *Etudes Anglaises* 17 (1964): 352–63, which I came across too late to cite in other contexts. Saying that "a study of all the imagery" in *Hamlet* will "prevent us from assuming that the play is wholly concerned with the psychology of the hero," Muir adds that it "may also prevent us from adopting the view of several modern critics" who seem "to debase Hamlet's character to the extent of depriving him of the status of a tragic hero" (p. 363). Lest it be hastily concluded that my argument puts me in the latter camp, I want to note explicitly that an integral part of my argument on the signficance of the show/play symbolism is that Shakespeare maintains sympathy with Hamlet and, concurrently, Hamlet's status as tragic hero.

INDEX

60, 110; and Rosencrantz and Guildenstern, 104–5, 169; appeal to Norway, 66, 122; choice of, 103–4, 174–75; dealer in "forged process," 4, 5, 37, 48, 88, 120, 138; description of Hamlet by, 102; imprisonment or entrapment of, 56, 57, 62, 90; in beast images, 77–81 passim; like serpent or Satan, 35, 50, 57, 95–96, 101, 103, 104; on manliness, reason, and judgment, 89, 93–94; prayer of, as "dumb show," 21; recoil of deed on, 46, 91, 92; self-destruction of, 104; and superfluous death, 37, 51; transmitter of defect, 42–46; uneasy conscience of, 143, 145–46, 173–74; varying opinions on his conduct in play-scene, 6, 7, 9, 10, 14–15, 159

Clemen, W. H., 164

Clown (First), 58–59, 67, 71, 80, 83, 85, 104, 122, 139, 144, 148

Coghill, Nevill, 168

Craig, Hardin, 157, 171, 173

Creizenach, Wilhelm, 161

Cunliffe, John, 161

Custom, 47–49, 57–58, 59, 61, 69, 86–88, 105–6. *See also* Habit

Dido, 113, 114; and Pygmalion and Sychaeus, 170

Dido, Queen of Carthage (Marlowe and Nashe), 170

Donne, John, 133

Downfall of Robert, Earl of Huntingdon, The (Munday), 24

Dumbness and noise motif, 8, 10–32 passim, 46–52, 111, 125–35, 148–55, 171

Dumb show: common subject matter of, 26–27, 29; definition of, 17; figurative disguise in older shows, 28–29, 30; forms and formulas of, 17–19, 22, 23, 28, 30, 160–61; noise in, 25–26; repetition in, 19, 24, 160–61; technique as comment in, 27, 29, 30

Dumb show in *Hamlet*: centrality of, 4, 31; conventionality and unconventionality of, 18–32; label used for, 12; as part of sequence, 4–5, 11, 13–14, 24–25; perspective on function of, 8–15; use of, as definition, 31–32; varying opinions on its use and value, and questions it raises, 5–8. *See also* Dumbness and noise motif; Show symbolism

Edward II (Marlowe), 162

Elliott, G. R., 162

Emory, John P., 158

Endimion (Lyly), 26

Extravagance, 63–64, 84, 129, 130

Fergusson, Francis, 163, 169–70

First Player, 115–17

First Player's Speech. *See* Player's Speech

Flatter, Richard, 158

Forgiveness, 143, 147–48

Fortinbras, 25, 66–67, 77, 94–95, 122, 144, 149, 150–51

Foster, Frances A., 157, 161

Francisco, 91, 153

Gertrude, 4, 22, 23, 36, 69, 83, 93–99 passim, 109, 110, 114, 118, 120;

mouse image for, 79, 91, 94, 98; reactions of, to Hamlet's setting her
up a glass, 133–36
Ghost, 6, 9, 12, 40, 44–46, 63, 82, 83, 104, 162; and ear/speech imagery,
4–5, 36–43 passim, 51, 63; dumbness and pantomimic action of, 10,
18–20, 22–23, 25, 31; in beast images, 79, 81, 91, 94; in confinement
images, 55, 56, 58, 59–62, 63, 64, 93; nature and mission of, 62–68, 71,
72, 73–74, 92, 95, 140–41, 153, 154. *See also* Hamlet [King]
Goddard, Harold C., 164–65, 173–74
Goethe, Johann Wolfgang von, 166
Gorboduc (Norton and Sackville), 19, 26
Granville-Barker, Harley, 158, 160
Gravedigger. *Sée* Clown
Gray, Henry David, 158
Green, Andrew J., 158
Greg, W. W., 9, 157, 158, 165
Habit, 58, 64, 135–36, 165, 173; effect of habitual practice, 136–41
Hamlet, 63, 159–60, 171, 173; pre-Shakespearean Hamlet, 6
Hamlet: admission and denial of wrong to Laertes, 136–41; and Pyrrhus,
110, 111; criticism of drinking bouts, 47–48; doublemindedness of,
on desert, 64–66, 146; dramatic criticism of, 3, 13, 58, 67–68, 112,
114–17, 126–29; dramatic practice of, 91–92, 109–11, 112, 118, 129–31,
143–44; imprisonment of, 56, 61–62, 72, 141, 151; his judgment of
Osric, 84–86 (and of Rosencrantz and Guildenstern, 104–6, 142);
his mimicry, 68–69, 84–85; his nicknaming, 69, 70, 80–83, 133–34, 166;
on habit, custom, and use, 47, 57–58, 69, 86, 135–36; on reality and
unreality, 120–22, 125–26, 135–36; his pantomimic action, 19–20, 21,
25; his practice of false-seeming, 71, 139, 145, 151–52; his rejection
of rule, 66–72, 94–95; role of fate in his tragedy, 56–57, 67, 103, 162–63;
self-contradiction or inconsistency of, 13, 39–40, 65–66, 67–71, 73,
82–83, 86, 94–95, 130, 131, 138, 141–42; varying opinions on his conduct in play-scene, 6–7, 14–15
Hamlet (King), 105–6, 109, 110, 114, 144; and King Fortinbras, 60–61,
62, 63, 122; likeness of, to Hercules, 83–84; sleeping and feeding of,
94, 106. *See also* Ghost
Hart, A., 158
Hecuba, 37, 110, 112, 114, 115, 116
Heilman, Robert, 173
Henry IV, Part I, 159
Hercules, 80, 84, 168
Herod, 132; and Termagant, 126, 127, 172
Holland, Norman, 162
Honor, 38–39, 47, 48, 61, 81–82; contrasting codes, 39–40, 64–66, 72, 146
Horatio, 23, 36, 37–38, 40, 42, 46, 63, 67, 78, 92, 105, 139, 152; as coun-
sellor, 66–67, 123–25; as "presenter," 31, 148–51
Imagery: beast, 35, 45, 50, 57, 77–106, 117, 149, 166, 167, 168; disease,
36, 37, 41–47, 49–51, 55, 81, 95; ear, 35–52 passim, 62, 92, 101, 126,